CLOUDLESS AT FIRST

Other books by Hilda Morley

A BLESSING OUTSIDE US
WHAT ARE WINDS & WHAT ARE WATERS
TO HOLD IN MY HAND: Selected Poems

CLOUDLESS AT FIRST

Hilda Morley

MOYER BELL LIMITED · MT. KISCO, NEW YORK

Published by Moyer Bell Limited

First Edition

Library of Congress Cataloging-in-Publication Data

Morley, Hilda
  Cloudless at first / Hilda Morley.

  I. Title.   88-2708
PS2563.087187C5   1988   CIP
811'.54—dc19

ISBN 0-918825-71-7   0-918825-72-5 (pbk.)

Printed in the United States of America

For Stefan Wolpe who put me on the path & for all those who have companioned me since.

CONTENTS

I   Sea-Map

II   A Thread of Scarlet
(Partly Found Poems)

III   Cloudless at First

IV   Give Birth to Yourself He Said

Acknowledgments

Grateful acknowledgment to the editors of the following publications in which some of these poems have appeared: *American Poetry Review, Beloit Poetry Journal, Chicago Review, Conjunctions, Endymion, Harper's Magazine, Hudson Review, Ikon, Ironwood, New Directions Annual 27, Mail, Menomonie Review, New Letters, Partisan Review, Pequod, Poetry, Sailing the Road Clear, Sulfur, TriQuarterly, World, Xanadu.*

Also to *A Woodland Pattern Broadside*, 1986 for "Not Tristan & Isolde" (appearing here as "Even Then"); *A Celebration For Stanley Kunitz On His 80th Birthday*, Sheep Meadow Press, 1986 for "Candles"; and *The Window*, for "Myth But No Sea There."

"So to Suspend It" (appearing here as "Even Without Moving") first appeared in the *Hudson Review*. "Deep, deep under white" (appearing here as "The Whiteness") and "Song of the Terrible" first appeared in *Poetry*. "Deep, deep under white" was copyrighted in 1985, "Song of the Terrible" in 1987 by the Modern Poetry Association and are reprinted by permission of the editor of *Poetry*.

My thanks to the Guggenheim Foundation for the fellowship in poetry (1983–84) which made it possible for me to write many of these poems.

My grateful acknowledgments to the Corporation of Yaddo, the MacDowell Colony, the Rockefeller Center at Bellagio, Italy, the Djerassi Foundation, California, and the Women's Center at Brisons Veor St. Just, Penzance (Cornwall) for periods of residence which enabled me to write undisturbed.

Special acknowledgment and appreciation to the Middlecott Foundation which helped make this publication possible.

Front cover: Grateful acknowledgment to Elaine de Kooning for permission to use her painting, "Bacchus #60" on the cover. Photo credit: Edvard Lieber.

1 Sea-Map

Sea-Map

Taste of salt on my fingers,
                          that's how
I like it:
            the line of sea rising
above the dark-green pine,
                          the sea meeting
the horizon,
                so always the eyes are lifted higher,
                the pulse buoyed upward
with them
            So it
should be for us all—
                      to belong to
whatever moves us outward into
the wideness, for journeying,
                          tales of
distant places,
                treasures piled
                to fill our smiling,
                              for us to know of
along the travelled coastline,
                          the mountains
we can climb to,
                each port,
                          each harbor
another window to wash our faces in,
                              pull us
forward
            & made for us,   made for
all of us,
            as the birds know, who
fly the continents,   the oceans
for their secret reasons,
                        a map of the earth
written inside their bodies,
                          marked
under their breastbones:
                        a continuance
of the now most fragile,
                        always travelled
patiently enduring world

Myth, But No Sea There

Myth, but no sea there.
Walls, blank heat, endless floors and no more caring.
We were never to be loosed by the sea.
Broken or unbroken the arches stood over the land
and the land heaved or not.
       What monster knew me?
Entered. Waited.

Unreconciled those fires crossed
each other, that steep falling
lost the world's bottom.
       Whose voice called a word?
With legendary herb, trefoil plant emblazoned
and sprung from the lion's mouth by roots
of fire: who clasp the heat
of earth's original honey in your fist: your dragonself
and slayer, heavy with season's resin and new weight
of leaves; clenched beneath you
stems break that stone and opening
lips issue in air.
       Trees
standing in fullness (no myth now
no legend) with gravity
preternatural, invoked,
freely held; become art.

The Mists Gather & Thicken

The mists gather & thicken
    & there are shadows
    darker & lighter ones
    for the night is moonlit
    Leaning to the ebb
    I slant sideways
    My body drifts
with the darkness
    It will discover,
finally it will discover
the shoreline
    It will return
    And if a voice
were to call out
   saying
my name
   repeating
what I should know,
    reminding me
of what I haven't attended to,
    if those words should
    follow me,
    continuing admonitions,
    not letting me
forget,
   it might be that it
   was yours
   or that it was another's voice calling,
   it might be that what has been
   impossible,
    should still be
   impossible,
    or the faint chance
   that the impossible
   may make all things possible
   again

Quayside, Ibiza, August

If you do take,
take joy,
if you do,
in the flamenco singer
at the wine-kiosk on Sunday,
is it possible
to look out at the others,
alone,
a woman   (in the naked
self?)
And they shake their heads
as my father did to a Hebrew
prayer   (the same movement of
the head, the eyelids)

They bring you wine for
that: seeing your openness
with them,
without shame,

also they bring meat, all
good things.

What is shaken are
the hidden places (the secret)
for us all together:

the coming out of
self is what I love you for,
Spain,
the ec-stasis, without which
you might be lost,
Spaniards.

Brook—New Hampshire

Mosses, ferns in the brook   Ophelia
one thinks of her
                    for there are
spirits in the water
                        as there are
bright stones
in the clarity
of this brook.
                Which Ophelia
is it?
     Sunlight
on the pebbles
                a wavering of
shadow   those small
eddies   the falls too   the deepest
places
        (one could bathe there
make this a stream for
living
        not dying in

I Begin to Love

I begin to love the beauty
of the old more than the beauty of
the young—the old lady shielding
her face from the hot sun with a black
lace fan and the exquisite
old man with the white beard & the old man pushing
the car of the young man dying
of dystrophy & the elderly
woman in black holding the hand of a little
child in an apricot smock

The Light Given

Above the 8th floor, Westbeth,
                                    seagulls
go spinning in the sunlight & the air
of January—first day
of the year
                A dipping
goes on there, a swirling
above the streets, warehouses, the dull color
of the river: a dark grey
from here,   red sidings
to the warehouses & darker
frames along the windows,
doors
            The space is bigger
here than where I live & I can
feel my breath & pulsebeat
rising with it
                    Not that
you can forget entirely, not that
even here where the air is giddy
& the light given to make me
smile with it,   as
my lips lean forward, so my arms
& breasts do also: the appearance
of happiness persists into
the moment after next
                                but
where is the light—
                            to dazzle
into silence,   or a whiteness
such as seagulls seem to
have here,
                illusory
in this sun
                    where everything
is clear
            or a movement flying
to wipe out the footsteps
that tread daily, nightly
on the flesh of my heart

Bathed in that Southernness

Bathed in that
southernness
                    " never
to be unhappy
again" *
                    after Italy
where each part of the body
speaks its own tongue and
                    " a man walks
down the street with his arms
waving "
                    on the dark
blue Pacific where I have
never swum,
                    the volcanic
rocks, red
and black, over
the restoring
sea ,
            small houses
chalk-white in the early
evening,
                violet and deep
apricot, or faintly
earth-golden in the late
day's sunlight.
                    The map
is moving.
                All day
the pure heat
                        blasts
the skin,
                the pores
golden,
                alit
with fire,
                each cell
a radiance.
                All day
those fingers burn
the flesh,
                making it more

---

*Quotations from Goethe's *Letters from Italy*

than mortal.

                A little while
the air is balanced, crystal
in equilibrium; a
transparency;
                for a little
the hour stands
still:
       the mind its own
pattern,
           breath its
fullness.
         Down
the cold comes
                 suddenly.
It darkens quickly.

Irresolute, Held Back

The promontory,   from Zivogosce,
curving down off the mountainside in
the shape of a dream that haunts us,
                                    as if lit up
from within by a radiance:
                            the packed joys
of over 20 centuries—
                        a lick of hot breath,
                                        the white flame
of a crystal brimming—an edge of fire but
shedding light still on this July day, the 9th, of 1983
                        News came to them
on the promontory from remote countries,
                                        the foreign places
a bold fisherman might travel to,
                        the air salt always—
was the water silky-soft as
it is now?
                Was it so clear then,   no oar,   no human hand, no
boat's keel could ruffle it?
                            in a greenness of subterraneity as
in those caves off the ancient terraces of Hvar.
                        The swallows wheel over
my head,   sometimes in pairs,   or even
clinging to each other
                        & sometimes one carries in
its beak a morsel of food for the young
                                    who circle, chittering,
excited by the act of flying,
                            trying their wings out in
a whirl of giddiness
                        Long, low musical tones are
sounded,
            perhaps a warning
                                Thrushes call out to
comfort one another
                        Westward
the sky lights up, ·
                        a flushed, a fiery light over
the mountains guarding the bay
                            A mist begins to gather
northward
                At the top of the promontory
                                            something

waits,   as it has waited thousands of years,
                                        alert to
whatever comes to it
                        out of this open
space of sea,
                pure in greenness
                turning greyer now
as the sky darkens,
                        a streak of lightning
flashes,   insistent
                        In the clouds over the islands
thunder rumbles—
                    the sound of the waves
irresolute,
                held back.

Is This Illyria?

Is this Illyria?
              I thought so.
              But this building
on the sea is founded on
an ancient well, a spring,
                          dedicate to
La Nimfa—a water-deity
                  (This hotel named for her)
                  The stream flows still,
                  the flowers
are fed by it,
                  are radiant
                  The landing plaque
commemorates the poem in Latin
                              written
for the nymph, her spring,
over fifteen hundred years ago.
Late Roman then,
                  very late.
                  But nevertheless I think
O Fons Bandusiae,
                          though that was
far from here.
                      Swallows chittering
wake me, each morning, here
                  & sometimes
                  the voice of a thrush also,
                  quivering, more vibrant
                                  theirs, calling
to its lover, perhaps a fellow-parent

The swallows circle & dive
                              repeatedly
near the door of my balcony,
                          uttering
cries as they pass
                      (as if to reassure me)
an electric whirring
                  Is this Illyria
then?
        The girl on the bus from
Dubrovnik—a beautiful antique
profile, eyelids carved like
those on a coin,
              hair golden,

mouth sculpted in a braveness
of definition,
                          might be Viola.
She falls asleep on my arm.
          I watch through the window
the rise of the stony hills looking
down at us
               with a thousand eyes,
                              each stone
an eye: lids stretched wide open,
pupils fixed,   surrounded
by dark-green fir-trees,
                      coarse-green
of bushes,
            eyes stony-grey, fixed open,
as if to say:
               redeem us,
                     avenge
our woes
           make restitution
for us,
        so there may be more green
& the graven eyelids close.

        The girl asleep on my arm opens
her eyes, awakes, sits up
                   says
in English, smiling:
                "This is a beautiful country
isn't it?"
         "Oh yes," I say. "Are you Yugoslavian?"
"Yes, I am," she says & smiles at me again

               But here, in this inlet,
Zivogosce,
          (full of us, the tourists
in hotels)
          the mountain
swoops down to the sea,
                  grey rock & little
                  green on it.
It guards this curve of the bay.
                     From here
no stone eyes are visible, no eyelids
fixed & staring.
            It is a wall
withdrawn unto itself

                    a shadow
                    watching
from a distance,
                        half-guarded
against us,   knowing that
perhaps we will disappear from
this coastline,
                    the northern barbarians with
their often greedy eyes,
                            their dullness
"dullness of the creeping Saxons"
                                their confidence,
the hard looks they (mostly the women)
give to those who are not of them
will be gone.
                The rocks on the mountain
will remain,
                the ten thousand
eyes of stone,
                    waiting
for retribution.

The Dust Covers My Shoes

They demonstrate against Pinochet now,
1984
        Among the people marching a mother
with her son aged twelve
            & the police arrest him
take him away,   a boy
aged twelve,
        the mother in bitterness, in terror
at what will happen
         In Ludlow, 1914, an elderly man
goes out to face the militia
a white flag in his hand
           to ask for protection
for women & children of the embattled strikers
        "Come close" they say,
"Come closer" as he obeys,
           they take close aim and
shoot him down
        I have seen the faces of the mothers
in Vietnam, the children, the old men,
           the woman
holding a dead child in her arms,
        or
a dying child,
        their homes leveled,
fields burned, driven
into camps
        I knew two little girls in Riga,
Galya and Bella (& Bella was very beautiful)
           with whom
I played one summer & 2 older women, my father's sisters
forced to dig their own graves
        & many, many
other faces I've seen—old men
leading little children, bewildered, by the hand,
the way to the gas-chambers
        & 2 young people,
very much in love, saying goodbye to each other
at the cattle-cars—they looked like Byzantine angels,
& the white-bearded patriarch
beaten to the ground & raising his fist to
heaven,
     & a small boy-skeleton

dancing to entertain the Nazi soldiers,
                              dancing
for his life
          I have seen them & the trustfulness
of beautiful boys & girls with rucksacks
on their backs,   as if they were going to be
"resettled,"   to work in gardens!
                              I shall not forget them,
                              the smoke is
in my throat, the dust covers my shoes.
                              It is a flute made of
their bones I use to accompany
whatever song I sing
                    It is the butterfly
who cannot speak,
                    the breath of those not given time to
form their syllables
that cuts my breath
                    It is those voices
choked back that make my voice so heavy,
                              that whiteness
a weight of ice that gives forth fire

Animula Vagula

animula vagula
blandula
small soul   o gentle
little wanderer

Butterflies aloft
on the mountain
shrines of Greece
breathe out their summer lives
dancing
in the sunlight.
Little souls dry-winged
as the plains of Argolis
in August,
sunlight beating out
its pulse,
            each butterfly
a soul, a heart's
membrane
            with no body

But now they have brought me
low   my wings
pinned back   my breath flattened
with poison
out of the sea,
                salt
of my stinging
blood,
the burden of
your service, Aphrodite

The Greenwich Observatory

The moon at the full in Cornwall
                              & here
in London again
                    round & clear,   fulfilled
also,
        by which time can be
marked,   the times of
other moons
                & always
time's measuring—
                    To be set, as
the Greenwich Observatory shows us,
                                to be
told in the lines drawn there: the vertical,
the horizontal—degrees of error
possible each way.
                    For the equator's
bulge,   the moon's magnetism
are part of it.
                    Whatever moves in
the hour-glass,   in the sun-dial,
is texture   is light & is
shadow.
            Waves of the sea in
Cornwall tell time,   making
distance,   making movement
by division,
                sun's finger dividing,
making light out of shadow.
                            Light paces
the hills in Cornwall.
                    Time moving
in coils & twists,   in
circling spirals,   descending,
mounting,   falls drop after
weighted drop:
                a measure
of fatefulness,   the past lived
& the present:
                time flowing
through the funnel of your cupped hand.

Cape Cornwall

That narrow path I travelled
off the promontory, Cape Cornwall
in the morning wind— clouds whipping
across the hills—
                    treading
an indentation in the soil, grass, turf overgrown
with moss, furze, bracken,
                            nearly
hidden, greened over & no lack of
herb-Robert, foxglove, red campion,
centaury, Queen Anne's lace
                            leading
deeply to the sea, bare rocks,
                            dark pools stirring
whitened in the crush of waves,
                            stretch of sea reaching
to the valley opening—a break in
the coastline, the peak opposite
jagged with the ruins of tin-mines
                            & I'm thrown backward
to my 16th year, to afternoons
exploring in a stillness of beginnings,
                            of
not knowing yet, a silence of singleness
still vertical, not merged yet,
                            ignorant
of fusion—
            behind that length of
hillside, golden limestone,
                            roaming parallel
to olive trees & fig & almond,
                            to
the dry rock sprouting wild narcissus, crocus, lavender
anemone, red silk of poppies blowing
dangerously near dark caves where I imagined
priestesses hiding from the onslaught of
prophets raging at the mysteries
they celebrated
                    honoring sea-goddesses
& sea-gods
            in that port-town
                            a coastal town, a Khof,
their rituals rising out of
that curve of bay,
                    shaped like a cup

held up to the sun so long
it cleaned & scraped my bones,

                            that brilliant whiteness
grained & made me porous,

                         receiving
in transparency

                 an arch spun out of
the air of Haifa,   dazzle of limestone
from then on,

              scoured to my vitals

                            decade after decade
to this day

For Bellagio, the Villa Serbelloni, Springtime

A hummingbird — that's what I should have been
in Bellagio,
          no rock there,   not a
little ledge of rock there,   no tree-root,
               not a twist of
bark, branch, twig,
             no tiniest slope
of dark earth there lacked
its honey,
         even the green leaves,
even the pebbles on old stones were filled
with it,
         no space bare of that need to make an
especial grace that suited it,
                no smallest curve of moss-banks
circling the wind of a road,
               wherever
the dark-green ferns & brilliant violets,
                  reds of
Christmas roses seemed to
utter the earth's richness,
           bursting
in wild pools of assertion:
            a declaration
that the world is here to be beautiful,
              to give
joy,   to itself,
         to make beauty undeniable
also for the youngest swallows
sweeping across the lake-lights,
             to cover everything
as our eyes are filled,
          to fill space up
with a million kinds of sprouting,   of
shooting forth,   wiping out
dismay   in that effulgence.
Even in the fog,   the mist-days,
wetness of the air, chill winds
             were other kinds of
grace,   gestures
away from sun-brilliance,
           extensions
of otherwise,   making discoverable
blue deepened endless

into hyacinth—
                    in the first primrose, fragility
insistent,   small flicker of
tenderness,
                    a morning star

Amulet

Ten stones hang in my ears
from the rocky coastline where my ancestors
walked (three thousand was it?) years
ago, on their way to the desert,
                              blue-green
as the gulf of the sea the rocks spring out of
                    It is
Cala Saona's color   southwest
on the Mediterranean island where I knew
Odysseus must have landed,
                              the rough inlet,
gem-like surrounded by stunted
pine and wild grape-vines
                    Color of level
water where fish travel
beneath me undisturbed, a magic
hardness yielding
no reflection,
              talisman
of initiation, amulet for guidance,
                              sign
of a bodily joy

Of Justice

                    That it barely
exists at all,
                    we know that
of justice,
                    that it's barely
here, in this world—
                    but the thirst for it
goes on enormous,
                    not to be gainsaid & underlying
whatever we fail to do
                    & whatever
we do
          O without it
beauty even,   the kind that one trembles at
or shudders at because it is final,
                              truth, even,
or what we know of it   are lesser
stars
          & this world   no matter
how true to what we need of truth,
                              no matter
how beautiful
                    in injustice
is terrible

The Steps

It's too easily comforting
to imagine all our thinking
derives from the universals: the good, the true,
the beautiful.
             More real to begin with
the harsh, the knobbly fact—what is
sharp-edged & most precisely there does
increase itself most deeply in us: the moment
of 2 p.m., this Thursday—
                    the uneven pebble
stumbled on, the acrid-smelling leaf crumbling
as I try to carry it home,   crackling
to dust out of dryness,   saying clearly:
indubitably, "You can't save me—I have
my own existence, mine,   with
its own limits that aren't yours."
                        That
particular leaf resistant to me   moves me,
inch by inch toward another knowledge
                            foreign
until now.
            The big words can be stretched farther
than their substance,   blown out with
air,   with thinness,
                  grown bulbous.
I can be lulled by them,
                  lapped
into drowsiness.   They can
bewitch me with what seems
a sweetness.
            But the bite of another knowledge
shows me what I'm made of—
                    away from
the grander beauties—as at Chartres
it is *this* antelope, not the idea
of it which makes for denseness,
                      a life thronging
at each level, those beasts horned or without horns,
one with wings & one unwinged,
                    the head of
a martyr bent half-smiling,
                     the leer of a devil
triumphing & how the ewe stands patient
her young nuzzling her,
                  each bird astonishing

for what it is—not for a generality
of form,
        as each leaf is etched,
                    sharp-edged
in autumn clearness—fiery-redness or
lemon-crystal,
        so in the crumpled streak of
fallen tulip-petal,   flattened
in my dictionary, or the unevenness
of a dried rose-leaf, creased pitifully
between the pages: not the perfect rose, but
these alive darkly in Scotian inscape—the truth of
the particular—this finger on the page
                   making
a place for thought, for me to stand on,
               to
look out from.
          That place chosen
by Abelard from which to argue
with William of Champeaux the Platonist,
               that
what the senses say is the foundation
          for
how we move toward the final things, just as
those single figures, man or beast,
            grounding us,
move us farther upward.
          It was the youth of France who
followed him, Abelard, alive to
what they knew as seen, touched, listened to, felt.
             That
drew them—to build their certitudes on
the tangible, on the immediate as they could hear it
           in
the white heat of argument:his dialectic.
          He Abelard, living
in what is manifest as particular, individual,
            lecturing
to those multitudes of students on Montmartre, the Mont
St. Genevieve
          (where in the late 50s a young minister
          from the Department of Public Works, ran
          down the steps with me, seizing my arm to
          make me run with him)
began to prosper from the fees of his young students,
             those children
of the rich,
        but lived in continence, avoiding women, whether

prostitutes or daughters of the rich coming to learn from him,
                                        until his desire was
set upon the 16-year old, "known for her great knowledge" & for
her beauty, niece of the Canon Fulbert, Notre Dame, Heloise—
& offered to teach her privately.
                            Flattered, the Canon gives him
permission for lessons any time, by day or night.
                                        So it happened
that love began to burn in them,
                            eyes drawn to each other,
hands groping,
            not for the book's pages,
                                moving
through the stages of love's progress,
                                "inexperience
making them more ardent,"   each act of touching
a discovery.
The nights filled so,
                his lectures become "careless
and lukewarm,"
                his students groaning
dissatisfied.
                His poems of love now, not
of philosophy.
                And the passion grows—even after they're discovered
by Fulbert, is wilder, more desperate,   a frenzy.
                Heloise, pregnant, is sent to Brittany, to
Abelard's sister, in his home-country, bears
the child there, calling it Astrolabe—after the instrument
that mariners use, taking the altitudes of
their direction from the stars.
                        Abelard has promised Fulbert
marriage with Heloise, but
                        How, she asks him,
can a philosopher put up with children's messes & their noises?
Only the rich can distance themselves from these things
                                    & the philosopher
cannot devote himself to wisdom if he is given
to worldly aims: as the acquiring of wealth.
                                She would prefer to
be his mistress,   in freedom,   with love only
to bind them. "Then will our partings make our meetings
the sweeter."   Trained well by Abelard, she speaks of
the particulars of marriage, how harshly the Church Fathers
spoke of it.
        But Abelard fulfills his vow.   They marry.
Fulbert is sworn to keep it secret, but tells all Paris.
When they continue meeting, Fulbert threatens her

so Abelard sends her for her safety to a convent
at Argenteuil, where she had gone to school.
        Thinking that Abelard has forced her
to take the veil, Fulbert, with his relatives, enacts
a terrible revenge, castrating him.
                                All Paris
hears of it & his devoted students gather outside
his room with groans & cries of grief, so that
the disgrace is trebled.
                        No choice is left to him now
except the monkish life.   Heloise by his wish,
becomes a nun.   He is commanded by
the church to serve the poor and not the rich as
teacher, having succumbed to the temptations
of this world.
                Finally, with reeds & stalks he builds
an oratory for himself & names it
for the Paraclete, the Holy Spirit which is the Word in
its beginning.   For the word only joins one particular object
to another, the word whereby one names, as Nominalist.
        "What we are about to grasp is always
disappearing
            into the mist or sun"
                            "*Speech only*
remains to people solitudes."
                Later, the oratory of the Paraclete passes
to Heloise, her order.
In their letters it is Heloise who is
faithful to his doctrine of
the particular, the Nominalist.
                            She denies nothing
of their love,   remembering   still holding
in her mind what was most precious
to her.
        Those legs & knees,
                        that throat exactly,
that chin, those hands & feet, that hair she loved
are not rejected,   not blotted out,
                            but
are the steps by which her love moves from
the single, the individual   to everything
alive,
        as those faces, fingers, serious shoulders,
backs of necks   those figures
sculpted in stone at Chartres
                        (begun 20 years before
                        the birth of Abelard)

gather in dedication,
                    glancing
past stems of plants unfolding,
                              leaves waving,
those thoughtful arms,   hair flowing,
                              fluted robes
making our eyes travel over
trunks of trees,
                    reeds branching where
Adam & Eve emerge
                    & the proud beaks of birds attuned to
warnings,
          as the mother-doe is, watchful
                              & the badger
alerted,
          about to set out on
foraging, each necessary as the antelope whose dark eyes
fill to brimming with experience,
                              ears spread for
listening.
          Swooping
they move us, all these gathered with us
into a space we climb as they do:
                              stone, light,
height, distance
               & closeness.

Eye of Pissarro

Let us begin with the eyes: wide-open
insisting on looking—
                        not to
leave anything out.
                    The years
have widened & deepened them,   hollowed them
into a darkness in which every point of
light can reflect itself.
                        By now
in the late self-portrait the darkness
is pierced, the light
impinging is painful,
                        no dismissal
is possible.
            Pain & acceptance
fuse into something else
                        & become
a clearer *looking*
                or perhaps
simply more & more seeing,
                            the act of looking
no longer merely "patience" or
"scrupulousness" (as the art-critic has it).
                                            The eyes
are an instrument, are a spade, or stronger,
they have made him into "a picking and shovelling creature,"
                                one who "delves . . .
into the tissue of things" to learn "to will what one
does not will"   to learn "the necessity of the world
which wipes out promises and is worth more
than promises."
                It is the presence of
what is there that he has searched for
from the beginning.
                    The eyes are alert to
what it is whether loveable
or hateful,   it is there.
                        The eyes fill
with it—weighted eyes in the photograph.
                                        Neither
do they dream—for it is the present they insist on: what is
truly there,   without receiving
what is handed down by others,
                            without allowing

this that is,   that is so,   of now,
                                    to be
obscured.
                    In "Les Toits Rouges" the trees beginning
to take quick breaths again,   leaves trying
to fly in every direction upward,
                                    whether
to one side or away from
the tree   —but not completely,
                                    for they are wings the tree longs to
use for flying—
                    Or in "The Mail-coach at Louveciennes",
                                    with the white horses
in rainy autumn weather,
                                    the road shining
red with dark leaves on red-brown earth
showing through the green—
                                    they are
of now, of what is real.
                                    Buds on the chestnut-trees
in Paris, Boulevard des Italiens, about to open,
                                    people standing
on the pavements, walking, drifting,
straying haphazardly a little,
                                    balance
for the half-blown trees.
                    The newspaper kiosk
with a domed top, rosy
in the mixed light & shadow,   dappling
the streets,
            a busyness
in late spring weather,   people
making a pattern,   as leaves do
in your landscapes,
                    spattering
the earth (as your eye finds them).
                                    But these upright,
sentient creatures are
interlocutory also,   electric
in their exchanges.
                    I could wish to be there, to be
everywhere with that attention—with your observing eye,
Pissarro: the same hand, the same eye,
the same patience reaches to the wiry branches,
to the legs, the heads of the Parisians strolling,
their flitting bodies,
                    to those hillsides

touched with blossoming
                              or to the scatterings
of people about their business,
                              and to the loneliness
of "La Maison Rouge"
                              Eye of Pissarro,
dry & tender at once, alert,
                              incapable
of omission—where everything
finds its place—
                    looking out of a face that has
"grappled with the world" (as Alain puts it)
the mouth dismayed a little,   but the eye
wakeful,   making permeable
street, hillside, road,
                         landscape,
as the world is permeable
by our actions,
                    that eye refusing
everything at variance
                         with truth.

Even Without Moving

So to suspend it
forever
              as she does,
the little Flamenco dancer aged eleven
with the flounce of her skirt held loosely
in her steady hand, to root her body
in one place: push it outward
                              What there is of
                              passion—let it
                              be suspended & put off,
                              do not awaken it:
                              Let it be held away
So it extend itself
              from close to
distant,
        into all possible
arcs & parabolas of heat
                              Let it not
                              be accomplished
                                            lest
                              forgetfulness
                              come next: the need for
                              forgetting
                                        (obliterating
                              come too soon
So in that kernel of
her body
        it be
held away, held up still,
held off
        but then
made more so
              from her body
on which the world can pivot
rocking   as it spins
                              To learn from her,
                              the little Flamenco singer
aged eleven
              who achieves it
even without moving
out of her place,
                so the little girl in the circle
of clapping women kneels, sinks down into
the earth it seems
                & the women,

they clap her, clap her on,
                              standing
in a closed circle in their flounced dresses,
the girl with her one hand upflung
loosely
in a gesture of surrender,
                              in unison with
what streams through her
                   & her left hand holds the flounces
of her fiesta dress unclenched,
                              but firmly,
head back, mouth open,
                   listening
to the earth beneath her
                   pulsing
to her abandon
              & all this
without moving from her place:
                         hub of a universe,
                                   center
that she revolves on: tautness
of position chosen
for the power received there,
                         all of it
within twelve inches
                   (as do we talking,
                   we two, in a suspension,
                   sometimes
                              staring,
                   listening
                   to a darkness turned to
                   burning
                   that consumes itself again to
                   darkness,
                              each time
                   more radiant

The Ships Move On

Freckles on my thighs, my legs—
                    I never had them
before (someone called my skin once the color of apricots)
the grey in my hair greyer,
                    grey to white even,
my face changing,   becoming
a bit like my mother's face
                    & I rarely
could see her as handsome
                    (though Eugene Morley saw it)
Faces of my women friends who were
beautiful when I met them,
                    so beautiful,
such promises of bliss I could
hardly believe they were real
                    or my face when M. said
"How do you feel carrying around
a face like that?"
                    Time has hollowed,
lined, dulled
the brilliance of eyes,   the perfect matching
of curves,   of mouth to forehead,
cheek to eyebrow,   the proportions
shaken   in all our faces
                    Those shapes which seemed to
exist only to please,
                    to pleasure
the soul,
          to make the observer
stare,   wrenched now a little,
twisted,   obscured by
sags & puckers,
                    hidden
by pressure of years: a parchment
where everything leaves a trace
                              I had thought those contours
on my friend's face hard & clear enough for
a profile on a ship's prow
                    Life has written
on us
          The ships move on
relentlessly
                    They carry us with them,   caged
in whatever time has written
on us   indelibly,
that amazing handwriting
                    (now only half-familiar)
on the skin of our years

That Stranger

for Moliére's Dom Juan

That stranger,
            that wayfarer encountered
by Dom Juan & Sganarelle at
the roadside
            of whom they ask:
Which road leads to the town?—
                        Around him
the lights of the countryside droop heavily
to darkness,
            the trees turn into
shadows.
            Surely he carries with him
a grain of truth to counter
all their searching for the ultimate
delight—
            a knowledge
or an ignorance foreign
to them,   emerging from a landscape
where the wind can be armor,
                        the sun
a weapon,
            the landscape of Rembrandt's
Polish Rider,
            where no bee of any pleasure
                        foreknowable
can sting him.

Matisse: Large Red Interior 1945

In the red room,
                    a window,
a mirror,
            a painting,
                        which of them
is which?
            Who can tell with any
certainty?
            The plants there,
                        slats in the shutter,
the animal rug on the floor,
                        as if a
foreground,
            the stool, or is it
a round table with a plant behind it?
                            is reflected
in the other table,   coiling
                        with ironwork
at the base & pots of plants in differing greens:
                        yellow—
& blue-green,
                while the black-and-white left-hand
rectangle
        with the big, mushroom-like
fecund shapes of leaves
                    & the quick criss-cross
of strokes to relieve the redness,
                    is there to cool it, harden it
& give us another,   an extra
eye to measure the whole of it by
                        It sweeps the red together
into darkened richness, smooths it,
                            turns it into
a kind of velvet-satin caressing
us   (our eyes)
                makes the sumptuous
normal.
            So we surrender nothing,
                                not the blue-green
fresh as sea-scapes,   nor the tiger-rugs,
                            mock-sinister
in their power,
                nor the apparent
standing-on-nothing that the tables do:
                            If not *this,* then

this (perhaps)
if not that, then
the other—

        The choices are
innumerable.
         Nothing
fatigues.
        Where tension like this is
there is joy also.

Birds of the Sun

I said: humming-birds,
                        I've seen them,
nothing could be sharper,   more
full of intention,
                 than
the movement of their bodies,
little energy-charges to support
                           the bluntness
of round heads,   the pushing
of beaks, hot-needled,   into
flowers,
           flowers of
the honeysuckle when I first
saw them,
             darting into
what was most needful,   in
unerring poise,
               a direction
infallible,   no instant wasted
                       For the Mayans they were
the birds of the Sun

"As Gold to Airy Thinness"

John Donne

Send my roots rain,
                        O warming
universe
            in which we lived together
which is warm no longer,
                            in which precisely
those eyes that moved,   the lips
that formed those syllables
precisely,   those gestures,
that voice with laughter, with decision,
tenderness behind it   move no longer—
that I may be tried again & again,
                                & should be
beaten out, as metal is beaten,
                            molten copper,
gold or silver are beaten again & again,
stretched & pressed out to
more resilience,
                a greater
strength,
            or if I were a
bronze bell   (brazen they call them)
                                whose tongue
strikes heavily but clear against
its sides, whose voice sounds,
                            beating
on the crowded air
                & sounds again.

Long Island Xmas

                            Glimpses
there were, intimations
                            out there
on the cove,
                openings
in the slits of light,   crevices
widening raggedly   trees
very erect   but nevertheless   speaking
to each other,   brownness of stubble-fields (Keats' fields)
partly gold, short-cropped   The woods
observant   knowing.
                            Beaches
distinctly veined, pebbled,
                            branches
charged with expectation   winds
always flurried
                But nothing
to hear: no voices—no human
syllable beside the extraordinary trees (curling inward)
                            Man's countenance
a blur, suburban   unequal to
the winds,   branches waiting,   eyes of the darkness looking
in through the window.
                            What conversation
matched them?
                All was extraneous,   a circumlocution,
touching on nothing
                    The cracks in the sky had light in them
hours later
                Our eyes were shuttered.

Advertisement

The catalogue said—
                      sea–scene
with surf   rocks   seabirds & in the background
a line of grey horizon
to the right: a scroll twelve inches by eighteen
inches,   should I send for it?
                              Or are
the words enough?
                      The Chinese cranes arrive,
perch solemnly on the shore   explore the seascape
and set the sea–air blowing here forever.

Nottingham Landscape

for D. H. Lawrence

A fresh, rich greenness I'd remembered
from my student days here (in England)
                              the eye
never too filled with it,   wanting
more always to bathe in,
                    leaning
into it,   sinking easily deeper into
a still deeper green of depth, as if to hear him,
                              Lawrence,
(even in the old cliché) "the country
of my heart"
                 a deeper, greener
than would seem possible, but is
here true,   greenness marked by
the darker lines of hedges,
                         or
a tree,   or small copses
of trees,   the slopes curved,
                         rounded
warmly,
          the landscape
thoughtful, lending itself to
thought,   the faces
serious.
              Even in the house where he was
born—Lawrence—so much is
alive still,   with living,
                         a lived life,
cared-for   & pride taken
in the living,   each object having been
known & handled with
an intensity of the-having-to-be-handled
like that,   with caring,
                              each piece of furniture
a member of the family
                         & opposite now
a pub named for
the novel placed in his mother's hands
on her deathbed: *The White Peacock*
                              (& any pub for her
the eternal enemy)
                    The girl in charge at the house
makes a speech about Mrs. Lawrence's hours
of work—so many more than

a man's.
              Upstairs the sewing-machine,
the black-leaded stove, the oven,
the tin-bath she washed her miner-husband in
bear witness to it.
              From that
slope of the street,   the dips & curves of
the countryside seem molded
to a human hand,   rising
to the Haggs,   the farm where
young David Herbert began to learn
his life: the work he was born for.
              My new friends—
met for the first time—show me
all this,   living it
from the inside, as I do,
                    so we can speak of
what Lawrence has made for us,   his making
become our innermost knowledge,   his writing,
living,   more alive now in
the air of our time   than
it ever was,   breathed in by us.
              In that landscape,
that city,   they flourish too,
my new friends,   & talk flourishes
with them, as it did with the young Lawrence & his friends
in Eastwood.
              A fresh greeny root plunged into
the earth here,   the stalks springing
above,   filled with
sap,   leaves partaking
of blue-greenness,
                    moistened
by streams underground,   wet with
the sea that England floats on.
                    A rib or
breastbone of the land is what
I touched there,
                    bones which were somehow
branches, raying outward,
                         beyond the limits
of any circumference to tighten them,
                              for the greenness
is not green only,
              is a flame of
all colors,
         or of
any color,

   but transparent,
        showing

its veins & turning
whatever rises in them into
a warmth or into
light.

Cave Painting

(In memory of Max Raphael)

In the Aurignacian cave they drew
a horned bison, black, small-footed, male and a female
hind, listening in gentleness and many elephants
enormously wise.
                Darkly, through holes, we see
not in light, but in sometimes lesser dark-
nesses widely pivoted, swung through them in a wind
the shadows flee from.
                Dry as ten thousand years
of white bones falling, drier the cracked leaves
piled careless as years and the wind shakes them
into time, heedlessly under and down, over Altamira.
There they lie and the shadows roaring
us out of and into season, time and over and cold
the year
finally on us.

Early Morning Music

A low whistle,   a chirring in
the morning, Holland, late August.
Some notes gurgling,
                    or rough as if
over pebbles only partly moistened,
                             some scratching
                             scraping
notes   (can those be seagulls here, 5 miles
                               from the sea?)
and a low hooting of owls   tangling
into dialogue
              out of
the bushes   It is the stillness
makes this possible
              && the long green stems
of trees on a sky often white with
dim sunlight,
             a few notes shaken out now,
tried out— a little silver box thrown
into the air in a small arc of
freshness,
            silver beads falling
into the grass,   falling
                    away, on purpose
to be dropped precisely
there.
        And why not
try it out, for a beginning,
                 beginning
of a slurred discourse, questioning
repeated, learning a few brighter runs,
                       the questions
more assured, even
in the wavering,
            repeating
the question, the exclamation,
the curve now a little bolder,
                  joined clearly,
attempting now a new level,
              but
not yet satisfied: ejaculation
emerging from it.
         Even the faintest of
vibrations an assertion

now,
       between each hush,
each breath,   intaken,
exhaled,   never stilled
completely,
        become
        music.

Out of Nothing

That time,   over 20 years ago,   in Venice—
I said: I'm on the track of a mystery:
                              the consonance
between men's bodies & the bodily rhythm
of a city riding on the sea
                         This time, 12 weeks ago—
it was no mystery, only a thread dropped once,
recovered now:
                         face to face with
our beginnings,   surrounded
by the shapes we had guessed were
somewhere,
                    hinted at, glimpsed
when we first came forth from the sea,
                              the amniotic
sea,   launched into
separateness,
                 in light
                 & screaming
our discomfort,
                    to be attached & not
attached,
            separate
yet never alone: How we longed for
that web,   those threads,   how often
mistaking a touch for a belonging
that was not there   & being alone
for independence
                     But here
in the "loveliest of cities"   all
is reflected,   given back,
                              related
in form,
          so substance
itself melts into other substance: the shape we make,
                                   whether
mounting or descending
                         a curved bridge or
sitting under arches
near San Marco sheltering
from the rain,
               seeing umbrellas flower
as Italian violets, pale lemons,
                         apple-greens,
blood-oranges,   to feed

our eyes.
                    What is reflected is
a part of the same curve,
                              related as
one stone inside the arching of
a colonnade answers the curving
of another,   the paired notes
chiming
          & even in the chill of
late March, early April   warmth
is echoed from these walls, these courtyards,
                                        gardens
half-hidden by wrought-iron
gateways,   from heavy oaken doors, their boltings
carved, eloquent,
                    the narrow passageways,   faces
of the passersby,
                  clouds scurrying
alongside,
            lovers
their rosy cheeks touching
in the rain, eyes alight.
                        They are a recognition.
It is the inner life
salutes the outer.

                    (Fingers stretching
                    make bridge-railings
                    what they are,
                                    our breathing
                    is air moving,
                                    trees branching
                    into wind)
I had thought—as I remembered it,
there would be space between us,
                              space flowing
as if at the end of a long scarf
                        rippling
in wind:
            buildings,
light,   the water,   a shimmering
& air between us moving,
                        but space nevertheless.
                        So it was, once, that time—over
20 years ago,
            when I walked with him here.
I remember from then   the cobblestones
& my feet hurting.
                  But this time

all is different: I am caught up—it is all one, all
made of a single piece
                         in a belonging
I never felt before.
                         I am inside it—an organ living
in this body of delight,
                         or a stream running
over bridges, along canals,
                                   joyousness
in the twisting grillwork,
                              a thoughtfulness
in carved windows,
                         in the little squares.
They make a network   & they fill me
blown into curves that merge with theirs,
                                             in essences
of dance-reflections.
                         For it is out of nothing
that we began—like this city,
                                   foundlings
in a reed-cradle,   survivors
in the bulrushes.
                    All our treasures
purloined on pilgrimages—
                              desperate errands
in irrelevance.

I Remember

       I remember
you buried your face in the crook of my
arm   hiding
your eyes the color of mine
clasping my shoulder
                  and all was gentle
moving with the light changing
on the sea & the colors
purple   dark-green   violet
enormous sky with the moon rising
heavy & close as your hand
& your wonder
that my breasts could be so white

Birthday

Observe
            There was a day
            for George Herbert
            cool & calm
            a sweet day
& bright he called it
my birthday
                the 19th of September
that day the Master-Builder made his promise:
a kingdom for a troll-princess
            There was sunlight,
quick clouds moving in the sky
            a fresh breeze blowing
& the chipmunks' holes
            were dug by goblins,
                            dwarves
            Observe the dragonfly
alight on my hand:
            its wings of gauze
            have velvet patches
It is made of twigs,
            two brown ones
            & one yellow
Its head is a mask from Africa
It is perfectly silent,
            delivering its message
Could it be offering itself
for my birthday?
            More beautiful
            you said, than any jewel
What we talk of has nothing to do
            with birthdays
On our way back the asparagus
            curves out its branches,
            shaking its leaves in a scarlet
            of celebration
If I am to be reborn on this birthday
it will be in the shape of a cactus
a small star, refracted into a diamond
to last almost forever,
                            repelling
whatever can hurt it
I will grow fifteen
            new skins
            over my own skin
so I can accept your gift of a cactus
without too much gratitude,
politely

Roman Winter

Cold stars the other night,
                         the sky cloudy
in patches
             Today masses
of light behind the rain-
clouds:
             a temperature
of autumn
             Let me now
hang upon the weather
for prognosis
                         and if the light-shadows
fall dwindling
or brightening,
                   either
this way or that.
                         On my palm's
                         surface
the lines grow & vanish,
shade darkly,
                   blur into
unknown curves
                   What is inside
                   masses & disperses
also,
                   is plucked upon
                   unwished-for
                   unforeseen
A pendulum   I swing darkly
dropping   badly weighted
backward to the earth-colors,
                   afternoon,
                                 clumsily
forward to a steepness,
a shaft:
             beginning
of a winter

A Voice Suspended

This was the year in which four beautiful
people died
     Venturi, Salzedo, Ferrant who was Lorca's
           friend
H. D.
The day I heard of her death, who taught me
the few words of Greek I know
         in a book with the names of
flowers in Greek
    & names of birds,
        I went to
Aeschylus, spoken in Greek
       Only the chorus
lived: crying
against fate, or speaking
for it,
   warning
imploring
     Over twenty-five years ago
we met
   Before it, on the telephone,
a voice suspended, hesitant, saying:
"I see very few people"
       But you saw me
Perhaps Hermes Trismegistus, perhaps Mercury,
my protector
     (perhaps our given names,
perhaps the herald's wand swung over .
our heads, mine ignorant,
       yours knowing,
stood me in good stead,
      allowed
this meeting,
    provided
sherry that you offered me—my first—
red-brown, nut-brown for
an English October.
     Perhaps he stood by me
then, though not afterwards,
       not enough
       Straying,
I lost sight of our patron,
     our defender,
of what he had given me.
     Nevertheless

he stood by us.
                    If summoned, he appeared—my guardian
We talked of foxglove, marigold in
the English countryside,   of D. H. L. in Cornwall
                              "How historical
you make me feel !"
                        When he demanded, you helped,
you helped,
              & in the solid way
without question.
                    To these four who by their example
helped me to cleave to my doing & not shirk it,
I am grateful.
                But to you especially
who loved my early poems,
                              though your counsel
misled me,   unintendedly,
                        Hilda Doolittle
like myself   American
in London,   blue-eyed,   a child of September,
Virgo,
          gratitude is now,
is always,   what cannot be said,
is of the present.

The Shadow

So little done, at my age,
                              so little,
compared to the great ones
                              & out of
timidity, out of the inability
to say, for so long—*now*: I must,
                              when I
think of Lawrence, dying at 44, leaving
behind him novels, stories, poems
                              & I
so much older,
              with so little,
                              so little
to show for all my living,   all my years
                              & so much
brewing always that should have been
written down, worked over, carved,
                              refurbished,
redone,
       as
I see it now.
          Behind the roofs of
this little town near Brussels—there are
hills, the beginnings
of mountains,   many trees
                    with leaves
of differing shapes & varieties
of green,   turrets,   spires.
The sky clouds over,
                    little clouds
appearing over the blue,
                    the moon yellow
last night, with a mist around it
                    & this morning
the shadow of a bird darkening
the sunshine,   flying
most swiftly where the sun is
brightest,
          barely visible
          but for its shadow
alive & gone,
          & disappearing,
a reminder.

II A Thread of Scarlet
(Partly Found Poems)

"The Glasses Would Stand Firm"

for William Morris

A man with a beard & dark hair
curling & flecked with grey,
                              hurrying
through the streets of
Central London,   through
throngs of people (it might be Piccadilly,
this year, '86, on a
Friday night)
                    his grey eyes staring
directly ahead as if he cannot
see anything, but seeing it all, seeing
everything (as Christian walking
through Vanity Fair, in *Pilgrim's Progress*)
                                    William Morris,
I think of him, his eyes saddened,
                              often
melancholy,   angered at
the uprooting of so many joys
                         & at our passion
for the machine-made,   yet
we mock him still:
                    that he created
what the workman whom he believed in cannot afford!
                         And how few
would prefer to return to handiwork,
                              the direct knowledge
of making (away from
the machine).
                    This time in London
I arrive in the wake of
a nuclear cloud that has darkened
the sky,
         hanging over
the city, even here, on
the edge of Europe
                    far
from the Ukraine:
                    misuse of
man's ingenuity, of human
knowledge & the discovery
of nature's workings.

                    "As a boy,
he knew the names of birds"

we're told of Morris,   by
a near contemporary (John Mackail)
                                how always
he rejoiced in the shapes of
earth,   rising & falling
rhythms of the seasons,
                                their intentions,
the way things grew or failed to
grow,   forms springing or curling
out of the deepest places—
                                "How I love the earth and
all the seasons thereof"—
                                who
wished for all earth's children a happiness
sane as the happiness of earth,
                                in a tempo
like earth's tempo of growth, of
change, sometimes amazing
in quickness, but slow enough to
taste the experience fully.
                                So he travelled
by preference on the waterways
of England: the canals, the rivers—
the Thames in the Thames valley & into
the Cotswolds, to Gloucestershire, to
Oxfordshire, almost to Kelmscott,
his home,   "house that I love"
                                to follow
the path of his belief & with a passion
for the work—
                                so that "the glasses
would stand firm" upon the table,
                                the dye would
print the colors that he dreamed of,
                                the helmet—
constructed as he felt it must have been—
                                sit smoothly
on his head, precisely
as he had imagined it
                                (though taking it off
for dinner was more difficult than
making it & nearly drove him
into a "William Morris fit" of rage, when
he might beat his head against the wall).

                    But brooding
without action was not
for him—rather the perpetual

making, continual learning in
rediscovery of what had been lost,
                              so those around him
were caught up in the doing,
                              imbued with
faith in it,   in him, in "Topsy"
(with his crown of curls,   so strong that
he could lift his little daughter by a strand of
his hair!)
            in his believing, in
what he gave to make them brothers, Arthur of a new
Round Table,   Janey
his Guenevere, Rossetti, his best friend, a loyal
faithless Lancelot,
                    but lost to them (unknowable)
as Lancelot was not lost.
                          For it was Morris
set himself to fight for
the driven poor,
                  "the working class considered
as so much machinery"
                        at whatever
cost to health & peace of mind, speaking
at street-corners, in all weathers,
                                    lecturing:
"I do know what I love . . . what I hate
and believe that neither . . .
are matters of accident"
                          travelling
to meetings, for
                  "to do nothing but grumble and
not to act—that is
throwing away one's life,"
                          spending
five hundred hours at the loom, inventing
new styles of type-face, six hundred
designs for paper, carpets, tapestries,
damask & chintz, writing
his poems, printing his Kelmscott Chaucer.
                                            To a
friend in despair he wrote: "the world goes on,
beautiful and strange and dreadful
and worshipful."
                  In his last illness
a piece of 16th century music made him
cry out with joy
                  so great he could not

let it continue—
                    dying
from having done "more work than
most ten men,"   saying
almost at the very end "I want to
get the mumbo-jumbo
out of the world."
                    The coffin, unpolished oak,
vine-wreathed, under a brocade that he
loved
        & willow-boughs on moss in
a farm wagon.

                    "Think of
the joy we have in praising
great men" he wrote
"and how we turn their stories over
and fashion their lives for
our joy
        and this also
we may give to the world."
                    The seemingly helpless hands that
painted, drew, worked at
the loom from dawn   making
designs, translating from the Icelandic,
printing, and writing
poems,
            the curly "topsy" head,
            filled with
the Norse sagas & dreams
of
        Arthurian knights,
                            the eyes saddened
by his burning desire to make a
happy life for the poor
                            the working-
classes, for all of society; to wipe out
Vanity Fair,   the childlike shamelessness,
the seriousness impervious
to praise, to blame,
                the honesty,
the dark hair speckled with grey—
                that man who
wept, in those final days, when someone
spoke of the suffering
of the poor,
                his body lying under

the willow boughs,
                    wind blowing
from the west,   the little Cotswold streams
running brown & full
                              apples
strewn on the grass,
                         the rooks silent
in the trees
                    a vine-wreathed coffin
in a yellow-painted cart
                         "with bright red wheels"

For César Vallejo I

In this, our time, a century of
the uprooted
                        striving
to find roots, true roots,
those they were born with,
                                    but others
which can flourish in new winds,
                                    under
new skies, with every
leaf & stem of flower newly
learned by name—
                        roots so much
deeper than they were
born with
                reaching back
into every age
                            (as Traherne says it:
                            "my spirit was present
                            in all ages")
                            & yet recovering
for ourselves
                a space which does not
enclose us,
                is wider
than what we know,   before we
                        knew it   including us & what is
outside us.
                Vallejo, you were of us
                even though born
before this century
                            The roots you had were
strong but something in them
hurt you always—
                        that one grows up,
grows older—
                        that tenderness
must so often be given up,
                            that so many joys
are dispersed with time,
                            that the face of existence
changes when nothing changes
                            that what seemed certain
becomes evanescent,   so fragile it can
cause us pain by fragility:
                        the heart contracts with it

that much, so much must happen
                              before
the complicated heart can find
a wholeness,
                    never to forget
wonder, the offering
of praise
                "This afternoon/   it rains more than ever/
                and I have no wish to live/   my heart
                "Esta tarde
                llueve como nunca; y no tengo ganas de vivir,
                corazon"
                              And later the knowledge
your childhood had given—
                              the fragrance of
tenderness,   a voice saying "Now boys—"
"Pero hijos"
                "I won't be away for long"
                                    the knowledge
which children have when they play at
hide-and-seek—of
the unforeseeable,
                    that in spite of
the terror of the moment,
                              or the longer
terror   which seems to
eat at our vitals,
                    in the end
                    what we know of
the tracing of a path
                (& step by step)
                                    will be
a clarity,
                whatever we were forced to learn of
the chain of sequences
                        (barely foreseeable)
ring after ring   returned to
their beginnings,
                        all that truly
belonged to us
                made certain.
                              Later (years later
seeing the leafy chestnuts in Paris
        "los castaños frondosos de Paris"
y dicendo
                "Es un ojo este aquel una frente esta, aquella"
saying "This is an eye, this is a forehead"
and "Tanta vida . . . tantos años y siempre, siempre, siempre"

"So many years and always, always, always"
There was someone there who said: "Don't be like that"
                              "No seas asi"
"You with your block of ice"
                        "bloque de hielo"
                        knowing only
your own ingratitude
                    and in Paris your poverty
so great, you hid it
under your greatcoat
                    "bajo mi abrigo"
                    "so that my soul should not be seen"
                    "para que no me vea mi alma"
"Lluvia y sol en Europa, y ¡como toso! y ¡como vivo!"
                    "Rain and sun in Europe
                    and the way I cough!
                                    I live!"
"¡como me duele el pelo al columbrar los siglos semanales!"
                    "How my hair hurts me
                    perceiving the weekly centuries!"
It was there in the end you were killed, Spain dying,
"Mother Spain with her belly on her back"
                    "There they killed César Vallejo"
"in Paris in a shower of rain"
"en Paris con aguacero"
                    "tal vez un jueves, como es hoy, de otoño"
                    "Perhaps on a Thursday, like today in autumn
"César Vallejo ha muerto le pegaban
todos sin que el les haga nada"
                    "César Vallejo is dead, everybody
                    beat him
                              without his ever having done
                              anything to them,
                    "le daban duro con un palo
                    y duro tambien con una soga"
"They beat him hard with a cudgel and hard
likewise with a piece of rope"
For you had learned the anger of the poor
"que quebra al hombre en niños"
                              "that breaks a man into
                                        children"
"tiene dos rios contra muchos mares"
                    "like two rivers against
                                    many seas"
"La colera que quebra al alma en cuerpos"
"the anger that breaks the soul into bodies"
And for the woman in the worn black dress,
                              with a bad knee

for whom your life had to make a distant curve,

there was
"no space/ Between your greatness and my last intention/
Beloved"

"no haya espacio entre to grandeza y mi postrar
projecto, amada"

only
"Two doors which come and go in the wind
darkness   to   darkness"

We did not protect Spain,
we did not save her
Olga, the blonde Russian art-student
in her red coat & myself

carrying leaflets
door to door,   saying
Madrid,   Madrid is dying

living always now
on the frontier of the not-done,

of the not-quite,
of the ungathered,

the fallen
apart,
      the never-quite-held together
      always forever & since

on the brink of
what shall not be forgiven

"y jamas como hoy, . . . a ver me solo"

"and never like today do I
see myself alone"
"la soledad, la lluvia, los caminos"

"solitude, the rain, the roads"
our half-begun, dying still unbearing
lives
        "tan ala, tan salida, tan amor"
    "so much wing, so much departure, so much love"
What we were forced to learn,

what rediscovers
us: the chain of sequences,
    ring after barely foreseeable
    ring
            returned to
beginnings   (belonging

"pillars   "pilares
without base or capital"   libres"
Something given to us

in our unsureness

"Fosforo y fosforo en la oscuridad"
"Match after match in the darkness"
"Lagrima y lagrima en la polvareda"
"Tear after tear in a cloud of dust"
                              to slake our thirst

For Vallejo II

In Zivogosce, here, Vallejo,
                        I read you,
in a country you didn't know,
                        far from
your birthplace,
                closer
to my own possibly Slavic forbears,
                                so they say
"Dobre," as the Russians do for "good,"
                        "sedyitsi"
                        for "sit down"
            In a cafe
among German tourists, I sit reading you
among them, it may be, the relatives
of those who bombarded Spain
from the air, unprecedented then, in Europe, 1937
                        & I, Jewish,
                        with a grief
that never can be healed
                for my dead,
                my tortured
people,   find myself
savoring their laughter,
                their high spirits
                & the eyes,
wondering, of their young children,
                forgiving them.
                Should you, César Vallejo,
to whom life dealt so many
terrible blows, continuously,
                        (I, too, know something
                        of those "golpes")
                        would you
forgive them?
                        For you these stony mountains
might recall the upper Andes,
                the cypress-trees, like spires,
                pointing remembrance
                If you could see them
you would give utterance to
that darkness,
                your pain lifted
into clarity,
                darkness
made clear,

the blackness
of a diamond,

your grief become

its transparency

For Vallejo III

What your face lives,
                is aware of,
                        on the riches
of your head,
              bent under
the weight of it,
              Vallejo

                And if the carts with people
pushing them, the mattresses,
the pots & pans, old chairs, or cupboards,
the exhausted faces,   children
trudging,   or too tired & weakened
carried on someone's arm,
                    planes flying
overhead,
           the ancient muskets
of the ill-armed at a bridge,
                Spain 1937
bows your head,
             how much you remember
of a childhood, yours,
            Vallejo
& Miguel hiding so that you couldn't find him
& began to cry
           & those "schoolboy syllables"
of your early schooldays
             How much later
you call for your sister, Aguedita,
              your brother,
Miguel   staring into the darkness
             "en la oscuridad"
How much later you ask them
not to go away & leave me alone
            "No me vayan
a ver dejado solo"
        & you are the only one
"el unico recluso sea yo"
        the only one hiding
before the door of the house
        "ante la puerta de la casa"
"y nadie responde"
       & no one answers

           Years later

we see the militia,
                    the badly armed,
                                        falling,
their arms flung out,
                    like those whom Goya painted

                    From the streets of Paris
"en Paris con aguacero"
                    in Paris in a shower of rain

amor ajeno en vez del propio amor
an alien love instead of your own
Could Alfonso not give you
courage, then?
                    Did he only give you
sorrow,   this Alfonso: "Querido Alfonso" with
his "siglos de dolor"
                    his centuries of pain?

With whom you shared
                    "un vaso para ponerse bien"
                    "a glass to make you feel better"

                    "y despues, ya veremos lo que pasa"
& afterwards we'll see what happens
                              But now you remember only
"la muerte de ambos"
                    "the death of both of you"
A stone to sit on—can't I even have that now!
                              So much darkness
                              so much *dolor*
                              siglos de dolor
But you enjoyed life "enormamente"
"Tanta vida y jamas"
                    so much life and never!
The love streaming out of you
for "the leafy chestnuts of Paris",
                              for the "sweetness
crowned by sweetness"
                    "dulzura por dulzura corazona"
for the "amada"   the beloved
in the "traje negro que se habra acabado"
                                        "the black dress
which shall have been worn out"
                              as honey out of
the carcass of the lion

A Thread of Scarlet

for Lorca

I

Huge letters—placards in Paris
in my student years   letters screaming
                        L'ESPAGNE

the years of "non-intervention"—

                        Older brothers of
my childhood playmates dying
in the battle for Madrid in The International Brigade,
the battle for the Ebro,   when the republic
stood alone,   when Madrid
starved, its people
begging for arms to fight back at those who
killed to subdue them,   women, young boys fighting
for Madrid
            Decades later in Spain, we recognize it, as if
we had lived there once,   known it as our own,
                                    the very sound
of the language close to our innermost pulses   the often
harsh extremes of feeling,   the proud stance,   the seriousness
corresponding to an inner history
                        Earlier,   discovery
of your work, Federico, in my student years (as the young men,
                                        fighting
to save Madrid, the *milicianos*, came to discover you,
as they fought for freedom)
                        Verde que te quiero verde
                        Verde viento. Verdes ramas.
                        El barco sobre la mar
                        y el caballo en la montaña.
                        Green, how much I want you green
                        Green wind, green branches.
                        The ship upon the sea
                        And the horse in the mountains.

Your eyes filled with colors
on the piercing edge of pain
                        even close to delirium
in thwarted love,   love turned
aside,
        love unfulfilled.
                A flight of

secret arrows in
               Lament for a Bullfighter, for
Ignacio Sanchez Mejias,   the grief cloaked in
pride: the terribleness of
what really happened,   the precision
is enough,
          all that can be borne.
The little songs, the ballads:

"Se rompen las copas   "The glasses of the dawn
de la madrugada"   are broken"
or "Oh, guitarra!   "O Guitar!
Corazon malherido   Heart pierced through
por cinco espadas"   with five swords"

The music mixed with grief—
              tongues of the five senses
stretched into darkness,
        into death.
            Spain taught me
knowledge of the olive,   the cypress,
          the wild rosemary,
violet color of stone on the mountain
stark-white walls behind palm-leaves,
         the paseo,
evenings,
      where boys & girls, alert to each other,
walked separately,   heads and skirts tossing,
         stepping
proudly as young horses on the newly whitewashed street—
          image
of the Virgin carried downhill,
       fireworks
for a patron saint's day—flights of song spinning
out of grilled windows
       First child for your mother, you're
spoiled by her, who had a gentle "almost childish
voice" At two months you fall strangely ill, develop
the limp that reappeared in your grown-up life,
         whenever
you were tired,
     did not speak until
you were 3, except for the folksongs
you repeated with your nurse & your mother,
        could not walk
until you were 4!
     How much must have been
stored inside you—those years

you could not speak,
                    how much "of the earth" grew there
how many plants, trees, flowers,
birds, clouds, butterflies, fountains,
clear little streams,
                    to stretch wings inside you,
shape your voice
                    The travelling puppeteers who came to
the village taught you
to make your own.
                    Sent away to school
your face grows strangely swollen—you're brought home and
only there you improve.
                            From your mother you learn music,
                            you draw & paint—
years later meeting de Falla you call yourself a painter:
A bad student, you got through school & university
in Granada,
            but mostly
you're wandering over the beautiful Alhambra hill,
the gardens of the Generalife   or
through the gypsy quarter,
                        the Albaicín,
            The whites of your eyes very white
the eyes very black,
                    & in that old photograph the olive skin
shows white, burned white,   not delicate but
bleached white in the sun
                        Later, in your 20s, you gather friends
around you, in Madrid,   brown hands on the piano, singing
                                                    sweeping
time into whatever shape you choose, nightlong,
daylong,   beginning
to write your plays,
                    your talks on
the poet's art, who is
                    "professor
in the five bodily senses . . .
                            sight,
                            touch,
                            sound,
                            smell,
                            taste"
                        to "open
doors of communication in
all of these"
            so the apple can have "the same intensity
as the sea. . . " you say at the Gongora festival where

Manuel Torres, El Niño de Jerez—great singer of *cante jondo*
(unable to read or write) tells you that
what he looks for is "the black torso
of the Pharoah," the Pena Negra you speak of:
"thread never to be untangled"
                    Black Sorrow
                    At one time you think that
you're longing for "a garden, a little fountain, with air, where
the five senses, domesticated, can look at
the sky and monotonous leaves"
                            but your life moves past
that garden, though your roots are in
your countryside,   in those people,
gestures of their laughter,   meeting of
eyes in partings or
encounters   shaking of those hands which
"have no other purpose than
imitating roots underground"
                        & even though you say that
you believe in "joy at any price" you speak also
for those who "protest against that pain inflicted
upon others" & in that place of your belonging as
few of us belong to place today.

II

I, born in New York, where you shouted
aloud in the middle of the street, roaring
with laughter "I don't understand
a thing"—often feel as you did and where you
cried out aloud, that night in Wall Street "I understand it,
I understand it now"   you, poet of the South,
"in this Babylonic, cruel and violent
city" in those nights in New York when
"Live iguanas will come to
bite the unsleeping men" I have seen but
have not dared to
speak of those mornings when
                        "the mind and the heart sink at
the sight of the coming day" when "the light is buried among
chains and noises" & "the impudent challenge of a
rootless science" where
                        "sleepless people stagger as though
                        just delivered from a shipwreck
                        of blood"
. . . . the Hudson rolls, drunk on oil."
                In that multiplication you knew,
I strive for rooted singleness,

                                    a singleness like yours, Federico,
even in a crowded subway car you kept it, standing very straight
you made your way to the door, calling out: talán, talán—
sound of a big bell & swinging
your arm in time.   You saw yourself as "so different
from those around"
                              & later, remembering
New York you said:
                         "if you fall . . . you will be
                         trampled on, and if you fall into
                         the water they will throw down on you
                         the paper plates and napkins
                         from their lunches
                         Gold flows there in rivers from
                         every part of the earth and death comes
                         with it
Nowhere else in the world does one feel
the total absence of the spirit"
                                        where
despite "an army of windows . . . . no single person
has time to look at a cloud"
                                   That movement of
your spirit, from gaiety to darkness, Federico,   from
spontaneity to thought in strictness could make you
say at 30 "Nothing interests me or
almost nothing"
                      Earlier, at 27, you had written
to a friend of
                   "passions
that I must subdue"
                           There was talk of
"sentimental crises"   of homosexual love
                                          "I seek my freedom
and my human love,   my human love! in the darkest corner
of the unsought wind"
                             Your play, El Publico, begun in Havana,
holds up a vision of the masks we wear, masks of
our multiple selves
                         To your friends you say:
"This is for years from now.
Let's say no more about it . . . . At present,
the audience would rise and keep the play from going on"
                                    Third in a trilogy
of plays on barren love: Destruccion de Sodom,   finished
in 1934,
              has never been seen.
"La Barraca," the travelling theater troupe you are
founder of moves to the old Roman theater in Madrid, from

the Alhambra to those plazas used "for markets & for
bullfights,
                    marked by a lantern
or a cross,"
                    offering to the people
"the very plays they used to love, . . . giving back to them
what was once theirs"
"the same play done two ways—old-fashioned, realistic" or
"stylized, simplified"
                         "We will take Good and Evil . . . into
                         the towns of Spain again"
                         "to educate the people
                         of our beloved Republic
                         . . . restoring
                         their own theater."
                         We draw from you, lean on you
for remembrance, we rootless ones, for encouragement, for
learning of you.

III

A yellow moon, pale yellow & enormous,
as we drove into Granada from the airport,
crossing the Vega,
                    a moon for
lemon-growers,   for orange-trees,
                              a moon for
gypsies, for the voices of flamenco,
for dances
             & the mountains
standing around us
                    Naranja y limón
                    ay de la niña
                    del mal amor
                    Limón y naranja
So through the silent streets, the early evening, up
the Alhambra hill   (unlike the New York streets you hated)
to that old hotel, named for Washington Irving, where
Mildred Adams met you, where you
played the piano for her, singing a new poem
in the old ballad form
                    "brown hands on the rough-toned
upright piano"
             They smiled sadly, gently,
when I mentioned you.
                    "The crime was in Granada,
                    poor Granada—his Granada"
"Federico" the taxi-driver called you, "I read a great deal" he said.

"Fuente Vaqueros, your birthplace—where the villagers, after
44 years, had erected a monument for you with scanty funds,
"not worthy of you" they said. Their eyes lit up
when they spoke of you,   how, as a child, you wept, when
your father sat you on a horse,
                            they showed us
the house you were born in, the garden
where the tree, speaking in the wind said your name
"Federico"   where you learned to know
each object as alive.
                    They're planting trees in that garden
now, the garden of your childhood and
for you, Federico.
                    How inward they become, in
pride of you, how serious their faces, Federico.
                                    Pain and joy of
your life, your death deep inside their eyes.
                                    These last years
children in the primary school you went to,
                                    where
your mother had taught,
                        write poems for you,
in this village, one of your fountains in its name,
Fuente Vaqueros,   even the policeman
shows his devotion to you,
                        lifting those posters
of you, booklets about you,   with
a grave respect.
                    We met, they met me, the young mayor
with the turned-up nose,
                        that young policeman
with his trustful eyes—
                    we met together in
our love of you, Federico.
                    All around us
this love of you,   a river flowing deeply
as if from time's beginning.
                        It was in our handshake
& in the meeting of our eyes.
                        Before that war there had been
your poems like folk-songs,   years of your giving,
founding of *La Barraca*   the flowering
of your plans
                then
the life broken off.
                    Later, we ask the way to
your family's summer home: La Huerta de San Vicente
on Granada's outskirts.   The elderly woman in black,

carrying a shopping-bag gives us directions,
                                                her eyes
lighting up when the cab-driver says: "Federico,"
her face assenting. She calls to a boy of eleven
to show us the way:
                        a country road, big trees, a path
along cultivated fields to the handsome country house,
                                    white-plastered,
green shutters over well-shaped windows.
                                    A woman
answers our ring. We tell her we've come because of you,
Federico.
            The house is much as you must have known it,
airy, whitewashed, a large oaken
table in the dining-room, good tiles & Spanish plates,
the sun's breath in them
                            & the two large water-colors
you painted, at the two ends of
the hall: colors
of an early Spanish summer: green plants & pots & flowers
in a patio,   blue-sky, warm-colored
walls,   air opening
under a luminous brush, broad strokes, wind tossing
freely in the leaves,   sunlight
splashed on the sky & running through it,
the warmth reaching outward.
                                Your room upstairs
exactly as it was,   the light oak writing-desk,
your bed along the wall & over the writing-table
                                        a large placard
La Barraca—from the window
green trees, rich soil of the Vega, ripening fields,
                                            mountains
encircling it
                (rock-mountains & snowy peaks)
In that room
                fullness of quiet,   freedom
to write,   to work in.
                        I learn Granada now,
set down there   on the Vega
                        "pure & alone" you said,
"which knows no exit except toward the stars"
                                        where
"the small object stands for the large one" where in your words
"Boundaries must be put to space, to the sea,
the moon, distance. . . . We do not want the world to
be so big . . ."
            Granada sits there in itself, complete,

curled around three rivers
                            & mounts its hill, hill of
the Generalife,   the Alhambra,
                            from which all
that is to be seen   is seen
                            Water, the little falls & streams
in the diminutive you spoke of, comes flying
with the speed of wings,
                            that rounded space
of the Alhambra hill concealing
a hundred secret wells—giving birth to
                                        lilyponds
                                        fountains
a fishpond alive with goldfish
                            pools
                            in which the modulation
of each courtyard is repeated,
                            each central space
                            a little bit
off-center,
            each symmetry
brushing the asymmetrical
                            engendered
by another smaller center.
                            Each balustrade, each pillar, window,
archway of the Alhambra   echoing
in height or length,
                            by indirection
a wider space   to open
a private depth,
                perspective
of intimacy: solitudes which touch
warmer than the public measure.
                            From what I know of it
there is an exchange of mirrors, a lesson of repetition,
                                        modulation
in your "play within a play" as you named it: "El Publico," performed
so far only in fragments, in a University.
                            The aesthetic
of the diminutive: "to limit, to reduce in size" is in
your folksongs,   the repetitions,
                            the refrains,
each time accented with
a little difference in the nouns which
repeat themselves:
                la luna, agua, noche, ojos, corazon,
cielo, arbol, la sombra, rio, mar, amor, nieve—
the moon, water, night, eyes, heart, sky, tree, the shadow,

river, the sea, love, snow—
                              they reverberate back to
the distance of lullabies,   cradle-songs,
                                        beginnings
of the language on the lips of children,
                                   those nurses' songs
you spoke of   which feed
the early tongue.
                   Echoes of ancient chants in
grief & praise, repetition modulating
to a simple statement (or so it seems)
                                        of
acts, of actions precisely seen,
                              one moment
to the next—a refrain:
                         For you, Federico, distillation,
at 36, of years of making,
                              each image biting down
                              each line a knife
in the lament for Sanchez Mejias,
                              torero,
                              great friend,
patron of the Gongora festival,
                              come back to the bullring
                              after years of absence
"Cuando el sudor de nieve fue llegando
a las cinco de la tarde.
                         When the sweat of snow was coming
                         at five in the afternoon
La muerte puso huevos en la herida
a las cinco de la tarde
                         death laid eggs in the wound
                         at five in the afternoon
¡Ay, que terrible cinco de la tarde!
                   Ah, that terrible five in the afternoon!
Eran las cinco en todos los relojes
It was five by all the clocks
Eran las cinco en sombra de la tarde.
                                   It was five in the shade of
                                        the afternoon."

In '34 they cut the funds for
La Barraca, your creation,
                         in '36 it's taken over
by rightists,   one day after
you speak of the need for theater
with a Socialist trend.
                   That summer
you're due in Mexico   but something

keeps you in Spain.
                        Suddenly
you change your mind.
                        Was it
your wish to be at home—only that?
                                To celebrate
a family nameday at La Huerta?
                                Despite the efforts
of your friends to keep you in Madrid,
                                despite the rumors
of an army coup impending
                        & your own vision
of "these fields sown with corpses"
                                you decide to
leave:
        "I've made up my mind" you say, crushing
a freshly-lit cigarette.
                        "I'm going
to Granada,   and in God's name be it."
                        The draft of
your play on homosexual themes, *El Publico,*
you turn over to your friend, Nadal, saying:
"If anything should happen to me—destroy it!"
                        Did the mountains
around the Vega call you back, the orange,
the lemon-trees,
                the garden
of the house where you were born, the tree calling
your name, Federico?
                        Your workroom in La Huerta,
the oak writing-desk,
                        your window
opening on rock-mountains
                        & in Granada
the little waterfalls
                which rush in joy
down the hillside of the Alhambra,
                                the streams rising
unexpected out of the earth,
                        the pools reflecting
secrets of indirection,
                        unforeseeable
spaces?
        Did they call out in
warning—those echoes
of words you heard in childhood,
                        even

when you could not speak?
                    Did they not ask you
to be careful—tell you to
stay away,
          not to
come back,
          to beware of
the night, the moon, the tree,
shadow,
          to keep away, not to
come home?   Stay
where you are—they must have
called out, crying:
we cannot save you,
                    neither
cielo, ojos, corazon, rio,
                         the sky, eyes, heart, river—
Their incantation cannot serve to
ward off danger.
               Stay away.
                    There is
a darkness approaching.
                    The people, like you, are
undefended, unarmed.
                    Already
it is late.
          Your home will not
be safe for you.
               It is
too late.
          Dragged out of your father's
house.
          No one can help you
now.
          The young baker
who brings you food, tobacco, a blanket
sent by your friends
                    can barely
recognize you: the large thoughtful eyes in
your photograph,   the nostrils
sensitive,   the determined
chin—so terrified
are you.
          And what of the brown hands that played
your songs for Mildred Adams on
the piano at the Washington Irving—
one sensitive hand in that earlier photograph
around your younger sister's shoulder, at

another piano?
                    Do those hands tremble now, when
you roll a cigarette with the tobacco
they've sent you?
                    Death has taken
your sister Concha's husband, friend of
your youth.
                    Death stands waiting.
"¡Que no quiero verla!"
                              I do not wish to see it.
The little streams run fast,
                              faster
down the Generalife hill,
                              the fountains
of the Alhambra rise & scatter
                              & the fountain
of Fuente Vaqueros, where
you were born,
                    where
the tree in the garden calls your name, "Federico",
branches tossed in the wind.
                              The sound is
muffled now.
              Se rompen
las copas
          de la madrugada.
                              The glasses
of the dawn are broken
                          where they shot you
near Fuente Grande,   before
daylight,
          at that village called
Ain Damar: The Well of Tears
                              there you lie
under an ancient olive-tree
                    with
three others.
              "¡Yo no quiero verla!"
              No.
              I will not see it.
              No.
The olive trees, the orange, the lemon
are shaken
          & not by the wind.
They shiver.
              "Ya los musgos y la hierba"
              abren con dedos seguros
              la flor de su calavera

Now the moss and the grass
open with sure fingers
the flower of his skull

"y su sangre ya viene cantando"
And now his blood comes out singing
a thread of scarlet
                    winding toward us,
                                        feeding
the earth we stand on
                    now
after fifty years.

III Cloudless at First

Cloudless at First

The sky cloudless at first,
                    later
the few clouds to appear
                        are dazzling white
through my dentist's window
the construction men moving up & down the scaffolding
with purposiveness
                    as if climbing the rigging
on a ship about to take off to
where?
        to what land?
                        Can we sail to
the country of brilliant goldfish—Matisse's,
                                a land of
bright colors   of boldness
where his dancing figures will never stop
                                & the tree about to
dissolve will remain forever
disappearing & rooted at once
                        for Cezanne has seen it?

Perhaps

Perhaps it is time, I thought,
                              having read Milosz
speaking of the length of his life, its phases
(and I not so very much younger than he) to begin to
think of myself as long-lived,
                              a long life behind me
perhaps it is time for that & I have been
shirking it,   frightened
at the length of time behind me,
the many lives,
                  differing kinds of loves,
roads & landscapes,   cities,
rooms, stairways—phases of
youth,   gropings, fears, wishes,   often
barely known—ignorance
of what to hold to,   encounters
almost fateful
                  & so many searchings,
wanderings alone.
                        But eighteen hours now, the company
of new & loving friends   & all this
does not matter.
                  A blue-green sea, frothing,
white anger on the rocks,   a vulture
overhead,   wild mustard in the fields.
                                    The junco-sparrows
reddish-backed peck at
whatever seeds, worms,   alert,
                              dispersing
to keep their distance from me on the fence-rails
when I move.
                  These slumbering, swooping hills are
buoyant,
                  gusts of birdsong are shaken out of
rattles—
            one fluting tone, then an arch of
notes,   a rough bracelet, interlocked.
                                    In the stillness
a low humming.
            Balancing the wind, the hawk
takes his pleasure.
            Something deep in the ground emits
a smell of damp bark,   a moistness
of roots,   of nuts,   pine-needles, pine-cones
soaked in rain,   something edible

to fill the gullet,   alert the nostrils.
      The ears waken
to the stillness: insistent
cheeping of a bird,   then a more rasping
bird-voice.
       While the emperor butterfly fans itself
on a warm stone,   this foot misshapen
by the weight of years can
mount the hillside.
      The span of years, a wave,
buoys me to this moment
           when I discover
           nothing was too much.

Equinox

                    The sun
is out   half-warm   the little
Puerto-Rican girl sings to
herself   the little boy has a ball
to kick to his father & screams out
loud in laughter
                        All the pale city
faces rise up to the light
                            We stand absently
in the sun or sit on benches watching
the balloon swing on the baby's
carriage & listen
                        while the transistor
radio moves farther
                        (playing
O Susanna) farther &
farther away
                        The long vibration
of a new bird's note
comforts me

Voices

That one could say simply
the world is ugly merely   but it is
not that only
                        the voices
in nasal Puerto Rican Spanish raised in
anger & next door
                        the screeching
radios   but there are
blasts of light from the rivered sky
                                        & the little
children in the back call out to each other
gleefully
                With incredible
courage like the newly born   the man out-
side lifts up his face in greeting
to the warm evening   the autumn
air   the light off the river   with a gesture
of old Spain
                raises his head & moves in a
rhythm of singing   a thrust out of
Africa   of Araby
flamenco

Praise

The hospital
　　　　　　beginnings
& endings of life there
　　　　　　　　The little boy
wants to see his newborn sister
Bent on a cane　the old lady
　　　　　　　　　barely able
to walk
　　　except at
a crawling pace
　　　　　　comes to see
someone very ill
　　　　　　They said to me:
"You're the daughter—you must come in here
to identify her."
　　　　　　"Don't be afraid"
said the Rabbi's wife—"it's your mother"
And outside, the wind & the sunlight blowing
each other in a dance. hardly ever still,
January—the Mediterranean spring,
　　　　　　　　　　her body
wrapped in a shroud　carried aloft
on a bier
　　　　& 4 men chanting
praise & glory to God, giver of life, giver
of all things,
　　　　　　giver of
death

The Tree

Seeing the trees lit up
now in the Xmas season,
                              I remember the tree at
the end of the quay in Ibiza
where the breakwater ends: the restaurant
named for Rimbaud—El Barco Borracho,
a summertime tree,
                              lit-up & shining those evenings
with bulbs of all colors
& we danced to the waltzes they played,
                                             our bodies
moving in joy,   with the music,
                              the smell of the food
                              the sky warm with stars
& holding each other inside that circle
of pleasures
              on the edge of the sea.

Café Guerbois

           Not the Café Guerbois,
but East 8th Street, a creaky loft in
the late 40s, early 50s,
               but a kind of fellowship
was there,
        a beginning
looking toward other beginnings, forward
to them,
        words given,
taken,   exchanged,
           turned over,
set against each other, lifted
to the light, examined,
              shared, becoming
signs of mutuality,
            tokens
of care.
        We did care.
        The talk, the being
together affirmed our effort,   gave us
strength
        "encouraged us with
stores of enthusiasm so that
we emerged tempered . . . with
a firmer will, . . . our thoughts clearer,
more distinct"
        Monet writing
of those early meetings in the Café Guerbois,
                 speaks not of
a search for meaning,
        but for seeking
of what can be made,
        made out of
the seen & what was
remembered of it.
        That was the time when
I still loved the city—there was
a caring then. It warmed, it gave us
courage.
        Each day our fresh discovery, a changing
revelation, a new act,
        as in "Excavation"—fragments,
beginnings & endings broken off,
           then juxtaposed
           movements

split off or overlapping,
                        the juttings
superimposed, a collision of
edges,   flatness swerving
into a bulge:
                the process held for a
split second.
                And now the cloud-edge opens
the air   making
a thread of flame,
                        perhaps
a woman's body
                        in greys & yellows,
shapes of sails taking off   & what can be
seen,   what can be remembered
of them:
                the unexpected.
                As when a cloud-streak
shifts out of a tearing curtain
of color, perhaps the beak & feathers
of a bird in profile,
                        out of which dawn or
late evening move into Louse Point
                                & the door opens
on the river.
                It was a great hive
sheltered us   & whatever was made to
shine there was lit by the sparks of
glances flying between us.
                        We were the kindling
for that warmth.
                Our breath, our voices
filled those cells with
a strong taste, a strange sweetness,
wild honey.

The Eye Opened

for Bill de Kooning

Blue & yellow of the sun & green
streaks that slash, spatter
flame
      on flatness
            & 30 years ago
the reds & blacks, brown & greys
cutting & delving
           The movement
tossing more now, but as
leaves branching, less centrifugal—
a web in layers,
        and
still that hilarity
      that I
can't forget—word I used when
I first saw the *Women*
        & joy in
simultaneity,
     the contradictions
      (I know of them from
that man who was dearest
to me who, in composing, thinking,
loved "the other side of the coin")

as in the knowing
of what is & isn't at
the same time, in a single
moment:
     worlds leaning
against each other,
      turning
in & out of themselves, there,
not there, dropping, falling
away &
    rising up at once
        as you said "But Nature
doesn't make me peaceful
      It does the opposite"
(While my love made in his Duo for Oboe & Clarinet the sound of
insects humming in fury,
      told his students,
pointing to the traffic on 14th Street: Compose
that!)
    And you out of

the clash of opposites—bay, roadway,
inlet,   green fields,   beach,
                              make not a
fusing or a blend   but an
enhancement:
                    the earth's bowels
stirring,
              where the painting
paints you,   paints you in or
out   & the exchange is
mutual,   is process in
mutuality,
               to whatever extreme of furtherness
be opened,
               the colors stretching
as when an eye is opened   in meeting
with another eye,
                    the pupil & the iris
beneath the eyelid,
                       as voices
may overlap   & for a moment, can
seem the same,   spring out of
the one source,
                  walking on
Eighth Street & University Place,
                              the eye opened making
essential fire.

The Globe

A plastic globe of the world
                              about 3 inches
in circumference
                      sits near my bed,
I've never told you
                      how in this last summer
I measured distances on it
with my fingers—
                      how far my letter
to you would travel,   how long it would
take for my words to reach you
                              (I've never told you)
feeling the curve of the globe from
point to point: America to Europe,
                                        Europe
to India, the rises & the falls
of the earth's surface,   mountains
& crevasses, seas & plains in the heat of
                                        summer
rising to the tiny line where my words
might find you:
                      ink shaped into speaking, loops
of my hand's intention—
                              the fingers'
reach,   to touch you
there,
          in that thinner air

A Thousand Birds

A thousand birds—they flew out of
your mouth at your dying,
>   as you said
>   they would
& bewildered me:
>   They bewilder me still.
Nearly 48 months have passed & the beating
of those wings has haunted,   filled
>   this room
>   where I
sit now writing, the room
where you died:
>   a clattering
of wings has passed through these walls.
>   Something has stopped.
>   Something
is unable to go any farther.
>   The wings are
>   still now
>   & I rock from
>   side to side
>   with the faintest
movement barely perceptible because I cannot
breathe in this stillness
>   & must set that power
moving,
>   those enormous wings
flying again

Letter for Stefan 15 Years Later

But I love life, said Varese, climbing
those steep stairs to your 60th
birthday party—his knees aching
(arthritis)
              & you, Stefan, your face set in
refusal saying: "I hate death"—
the 2 of you—most gifted
of all the men I've known in making
life more alive,   more charged with
pride.
           It has been
a long journey to arrive at
this place,   many faces, voices filling
the road to it—Swedish, Indian, Dutch, Chinese.
                            Unbroken
as a heart-beat the sound of waves here,   or timed as
the lungs exhaling breath, indrawing it,
                      the sea moving,
sighing, gasping,   roaring
sometimes over torn aprons of
foam,
            hills falling
moss-green to the sea, rocks fierce as the outline of
castle-ruins in this sharpened air, fields hanging
in a crystal space,
                edged & clear where sun lights up
the dark clouds unexpected,   a red motorboat tilts & veers,
                              a sailboat
poised whitely in dark water sets off those houses' whiteness
until a sweeping arch—extravagant in
promise—a rainbow
one foot in the waves, the other
on the hill,   insistent, waiting
for nearly thirty minutes,
                  as you stood once, your arms
flung out, your eyes dissolving
fear,   even here, now,   where there is no home except in
writing   lighting up the 19th of July, 1987,
         today.

A Hundred Lessons

Having known at 18 that I would always
go through,   into
                    & never away from—or
past what confronts me,
                         deep into
the darkest places,   blackest,
muddiest of pools, most dangerous even,
                                   never
to skirt them,
               I do so still, even now,
again & again
               in spite of knowing that I shall
                                    have to
drag myself out by main force & walk away—
& find still that voice on the telephone
my brother, knowledge of my belonging in
some nowhere,   some no place
                         And are you not for me
a snare still,   a delusion,
                         after
2 years & more, even now,
                         that voice
on the telephone saying: my life is
rootless,   empty?
               Am I a Desdemona
to be beguiled by pity for one
who goes through dangers wilfully
                         —& learning
nothing from them
                    "and she did pity them"
repeats the injury
                    which he calls
"pleasure" till he is jaded
by it?
     I know better,   having learned
a hundred lessons
                    For am I not
of that tribe that crossed
the plains where the houses
were made of mud
                    & through
the desert to a strip of land
along the sea?
               And have I not seen those
heavy blocks of stone, the Gate of the Lions

at Mycenae?
          Of that mud
out of the blackest pool, that
dark, sweet earth shall I build
my blocks of stone,
                    a building
where the door is for going through,
kept open,
          & whatever is
is not to be circumvented,
                              is to be entered,
behind which there is always
each time
          a new place

The Rose

They sent red roses, a dozen
for your birthday
     (the fifth one
since your death)
     half-opening buds, dark-red,
        exactly
what you'd have chosen
   if you had the choice,
     to make your spirit
smile, to give you pleasure,
      to win from you
recognizance (your eyes softened,
    your face flushed a little)
Dark-red buds
   they opened
steadily, without misgivings
or excess of caution
     Only one was hesitant—
I moved them all to the light,
      so the slow one turned
directly to the window, facing
the light & slowly,
    the next day
    a petal lifted
on its side, then more so,
     then another,
then more beneath, gently pushing outward
invisibly (so gradual the movement)
& in the end that flower was richer, heavier &
deeper-colored then the others, luxuriant as they were not,
      more—
not-to-be-daunted
    As the others crumpled,
withdrew themselves,
    it held itself still open & even
decaying filled the air with a particular
sweetness,
   a royal redness

The Shirt

No leaf moves. The weather
hangs in a daze.
                    Scarcely a bird-call.
By what am I pierced?
                        The sharp point of
what instrument drills through me?
There was a blue short-sleeved shirt
    I bought for you
one summer,
               with beautiful long bone-buttons
made for frog-fastenings.
You loved & wore it till the threads showed
white from wear:
               I can see nothing else but
this & the shape of your neck rising
out of the collar & your head—the oval
"of a second-century man" as Olson saw it,
                   & your hands
short-fingered with black hair on their backs.
              Nothing
is clear to me except the smell of you
    & the feel
of your skin

Pomegranates

My chin is stained with the dark-red
pomegranate juice
This autumn I have eaten pomegranates
knowing their seeds were symbols
of a rebirth
       All night we were close to death
All night death lived with us
       We have been living death
       too long now
How many months is it?
I have walked often along the river
evenings   face wet   my hands in my pockets
staring at the late sunset & the haloed lights
of boats moving slowly
stately in the fog
          beyond all misery
relentless

Fisherman

On the beach at Cullera,
                  he is
conscious of one thing only—
                            a thousand
shells lie there, delicate & alert;
                                mountains
are baroque distractions;
                        a sail from the fish-
ing fleet in Cullera breaks up
the blue-green hemisphere
                          But not for him
He sees only the fish sliding
in the waves at the possible
angle of light & shade he has
calculated to an inch,
                    the net on his arm as much
a part of his body as eye, ankle-bone or
wrist,
      with a flick of movement,
net's swing, arch turning,
                  curve of
hand, feet, shoulders, deliberateness
of stance:
            these leap where the fish does,
retreat, as the wave recedes,
                   subsiding
with the ebb of the sea

The Lizard

The lizard's heart throbs
faster than mine through his
green spots.
    With prehistoric
claws he seeks his shelter
in the shadow of the vine,
       his head
to one side in watchfulness.
        Measure it:
observe the suspense. He is
anchored to it—the fear of danger—& we are
anchored to nothing.
     Though the Spaniard finds
in San Juan Bautista's effigies his satisfaction
without knowing why,
      we seek out the mystery: to learn
         to care
and how much,
     for even the bicycle
on the white wall may be a glyph
        and magical.
     But my heart
beats slower than the lizard's,
       making
the dead to rise up
     weeping
our own tears to bewilder us.

Tolstoy's Anna

Anna, the small curls on the nape of her neck
                                    elastic
with energy,
                     the smile forming itself on her mouth
without her knowing it,   in sheer pleasure of
living,   her grey eyes tender,
                              who wanted nothing
except to love
                 & cared nothing even
for the world that is made by loving,
                                could not
recognize it even when it was almost there for her,
                       wanting
her life to be composed of nothing but
love, the love of a man,
                  to be filled only
with that   & with the love of her son Seryozha,
                          unable
to make of the dailiness of love a world in which
to stretch herself
               & putting
her pride always where it could
hurt her most—all her gifts of imagination used
only as sorry substitutes,
                  impatient
with what was given her,
                  longing
to live & knowing no other way except by means of a
passion— & that demonstrated perpetually,
                            her energies
torn always on the horns of a dilemma, wishing,
as she says, to be forever The Mistress,
the caressed one,
                the abyss yawning for her
in frightfulness when love asks to be saved
                     & what she longs for
is without conditions,
                unfitting her
for what would not destroy her

For Margharita Rospigliosi

That light step,
                    that dancing walk
we heard & the body borne forward
as if with a breeze behind it,
                              that voice
tempered & warm,
                        or golden-bronze as
a swung bell in a tower
                          & by
the warmth of her recognitions
                                where the courtyard
bore the tracings of
her steps crisscrossing—a passage
directed as a bird's flight
                          Margharita
if you were a princess also,
a Rospigliosi that was only
a small speckle of gold-dust about you,
for it was what you understood,
                                what you could
make happen, that counted most
                              & the Roman ground
we touched when you led us
on our errands,   searches,   hived
with treasures rich as the textures
of your voice.
                    How deeply
we sank into that harbor,
that haven you made for us—
                              the dark-rosy
city swirled below us.
                          If I returned
even now, alone   & without him—
the walls would shine.
                          What were shadows
would warm me still   protecting
the spaces you built for us,
                              to work and
think in. The air
charged with your answers.

Paris

That world where no one
is other than what
he emerges as   (from the vibration
                    of others
& is what he is to himself because of
a juncture of moving causes   is
as the streets of Paris unfold out of
other streets (Rue Jacob from Rue de Seine and it
                    from St. Germain
and remove their other skins (the bulbs of tulips, irises
                                but differently)
out of one distinct form into
another, where by the spark circling (a word, a tone
                                        of voice, a smile,
                                        a look specially
                                        pointed)
the mind is filed down   (fined) into a
plunging will of itself driving
through tunnels (waves)
that world where no one
lets the window swing to
or light blur on the shield   so an edge of the mind
                            sharpens (to impulse
when laughter reaches a pitch   when it brims over
into intelligence

One Voice

Sundays
        walking on Hampstead Heath I heard it:
that enormous sound—the Welsh miners,
having marched from Wales to London,
singing,
        breaking
into the silence, as a sea rising
breaks on cliffs & headlands
                    made of
rocks & stone enough to
split them open,   bring the piled-up
flint & granite
crashing   splitting open
the quiet of the day—up Heath Street
to the pond & Jack Straw's Castle,
                    where they
massed singing:
        one voice.

The Coin

Splashing of wings
in the air
         all day
the insistent messages
             La belle phrase
coupée
        the newly-minted coin
taken out to shine
in the sun
        again & again

Hedda

A fine snow falling
quickly. Crystals.
Crackling underfoot.
                              A season
for bonfires   fires in the light
wind   (move, move faster

            As cold as Norway
where she strode up & down
the garden
                              All fences
down inside her,   nothing
to burn but paper
in the blowing
of the light wind
                              A wasting
of swiftness
away,   spattering
of pistols in a garden
knotted with fences
                  Tinsel of vine-leaves
& the wreath awry
                        Dark   dark rotting
of garlands in the mud
                              Dark,
dark the wreath uncoiling
in redness   the frozen hair

The Gift

I would wish to give you
again
        whatever (everything
I have given you
& not take any of it back

I would wish to tell you
all the good things I have told you
again & again   & not stop to
wonder if you are there to listen (or not)
I should like to bring you
                      for tomorrow
something completely new,
                something
you never knew existed,
              something
quite different from
anything you've thought of,
up to now,
            (whatever you've thought of
when my name happened to occur to you

Sheep Language

What have I done that I should find myself
here, in this meadow
                   in the Cotswolds,   sheep bleating
(from time to time) on the other side of
the fence,
        hurrying away
from the drinking-trough as I pass,
                        so I feel
their peace infringed upon
                    (& I the cause of it)
that peace their drowsy presence overfills to brimming,
Keatslike,   almost more than I can hold
                        But I hold it
as if in a waking dream,   the spell is
upon me   & out of it
my voice can speak   & speaks as
it must   in accents only they
can understand:
           a voice for them,
                   speaking
as they need to hear it,
              have heard it
centuries ago—sheep-language—
            I must have
stood here & found the sequence
of words,   the phrase,
            the cadence
formed for their ears,
           for the rhythm
of their nuzzling,
their nudging movements
             & I, a speaker
of first-generation English,
            who recognize the knights
in stained-glass windows
            in the village churches
of Gloucestershire which William Morris loved,
            those knights
who cut my Jewish forefathers down, setting out
for the Crusades,
        these little churches built, as
               Morris saw them
in joyful dedication,
        out of love.

Song of the Terrible

Finally, the fire went up,
                    when I'd
ceased to worry it,
                    given up
entirely on it,
               rinsing
my eyes of smoke-tears,   my fingers
of soot-smudges
                    & turned away completely
                    Finally then, it took, & as
the smoke cleared, my head & eyes clearing
with it   heart lightened,
& I saw the dark-red colored
wine-dark leaf I'd chosen to
save for you, deep-red as
the heart is in its veining & even
shaped like a heart as well:
the darkest red in the center—
but winged, in the form of a message,
                                   & I was
reminded of the time when, sewing,
I pricked my finger   & the crimson
blood of my heart appeared on
the skin's surface & I thinking:
I should be making a song for you
like the kind they used for ballads
when they said: Love, I love—I love you
& what was terrible
was simple

Warmth of This Night

Warmth of this night:
                         Here the sea
offers itself,
            offering
so much
          The white presences
entering a half-light & twelve years
ago—that beach
that tower watching,
                   the stars funneling
downward   or three years back
those nights for not unhappy
sleeplessness   for breathing
as the air   air itself
breathed   as the sky over the sea took on
a color to recognize:
                for all the wakeful
a reassurance
           & purple
for a bird raising its head,
                  because it was
time, high time
to speak,   to make itself
known
against the morning

Even Then

Not Tristan & Isolde,
                    not Heloise
and Abelard,
                    not love in
tragedy,   or the dying away into
love only,
               & even when
you would say, at the Greek florist's
on the corner of 72nd Street: I want a rose for
my rose of a woman (looking
at me)   it was not only *that*
you meant,
                  but rather, for us, somehow, even
with our arms plunged to the elbows in
the gravel of daily living,
                         for us to flower
even then,
             to make—
in that harshness, that effort,
                                     even
in that straining—
                    a garden
and not to live richly only,
                             but
to give that richness back.

Paseo Hour

Light's whiteness
                    Ibiza
port of plumaged doves' reflection
trembling in pearl
                        horizon of
light & stillness
                        The water too is
light
        light under the sky in which all heads
                                all
hands are poised   So time
quivers   times' reflection on the island's
coves   the rock
                    the walls'
whitewash   towered clock
                            Whiteness
deepens   a crystal
                        gradually
darkening
            growing
darker

Under That Dark

From the plane window, mid-Atlantic,
a pink-purple flush of light ahead of us.
Who said, "I want to cross the ocean
with you?"
                    Who was it, spoke like that
over 30 years ago?
                    (Where is he?)
What dive into the unknown took him, years
after shadows covered our desiring,
darkening the clasp of
our hands,
                    by which I am
darkened still.
                    This winter
darkens us all.
                    How many,
                    how helpless
the many of us
                    & the gamblers gamble
short-sightedly, with all
the helpless,
                    with the most helpless
most of all.
                    The purple-pink flush of
Aurora's face   ahead of us   holds me
to you still.
                    Are there any
surprises left,   equal to
that surprise you showed
when you fell?
                    Was it out of
her hands you fell,   Aurora's,
your face flushed with her color,
                                        ears
warm still?
                    Our handclasp
pressed more tightly than ever
together
under that dark

Yeats at Seventy

The impossible: as the wild
blackberry blossom blown frostily
on the deep hedge, the azalea offers
fragility
in awesomeness
              while I am
thrust out of my eye which meets
the flashing tanager
              or knots itself
in a cloud.
        There is
a signal between watcher and thing seen:
                    that communication
which has always been left out.
                I bend the dark sky
curving with light nearest the sun
                and star-signs
of continuous expansion.
           With music sounding
the sand takes shape on parchment
              and words
under pressure of thought.
           An act of faith, he said,
is what we aim at: an impossible
aim:
       The nasturtium
blue out of the earth,
          the clematis
take action after much thought.

Out of Blackness

Rocks brown-golden in
this light, this summer evening, Cornwall,
whether of the sea or of the hillside
>   They have
had their color a long time,
embedded.
>   The green hill indented
behind them is alive, porous.
>   The sun has seeped
into each grain, each hollow
possible. It withholds
nothing.
>   The light it faces is
no different from the hill itself.
>   Waves lift.
>   They splash
in white around the rocks,
small bursts of energy,
of dancing
>   more wildly
where the rocks are black, jagged
in a blackness of anger,
fury of long-standing—several
thousand years when others
such as I am have stared at them
accepting
>   as the hillside
accepts, aware,   draws to itself greenness
counter to its own,
>   a restlessness,
a rising out of blackness   where nothing
is accepted.

Well of Sancreed

The dark-green richly smelling
well of Sancreed, Cornwall,
                              shadowy, nearly
buried, fed underground these several
thousand years,   the narrow trail leading
to it
     "It's the smell I love there" said Joan
the milk & egg lady, born near it
                              "And why don't they
have Maypole dances any more?" nodding to me   as if
I should understand
                 Which I do, for it had
every kind of rich, delight-offering
smells, dark & tangy,
                         spicy,
deep-rooted,
             coming
from the farthest places,   the richly-smelling
Orient,   also from close by—
the startling freshness,
                         sweetness
for the most delicate nostrils
                         Never to leave it
would be best, we thought,   to stay on
rooted in that tangle,
                         the nails of our feet & fingers
nourished and the pores of our skin
                              clothed & fed by it
we would be   & thickly covered,
                         a few days, a week perhaps
2 weeks there   equal
to centuries

Elegy II

Disappeared.
Suddenly not there.
Not in trees
cows, houses, birds, bushes, dogs, plants left
behind.
As that white cloud
purer than any soul
whiter
than snow disdains us not
but moves
behind the Norway spruce and will not
(out of this summer) let us fall,
is
there in light we cannot feel, but
blown upon is torn, dissolves
and through our lack of care
blots
out—
bequeaths us loss
in place of
that safety
we failed to know of
giving.

The Castle, Elsinore

Great empty rooms,
                    out of long windows
the light blue sea: the Sund between Sweden
& Denmark,   a few, very few
pale clouds,   long tables in the center
the elegant simple chairs,
                             eloquent
in grace   On the wall—portraits.
                                  Chandeliers
hang from the ceiling,   as made for us,
joyfully,   to play with
                 & yet, in all this fittingness
for our delighting—
                  an emptiness—
                        as Traherne
has it, "the moving jewels"
                  are
absent—the men, the women
in festive garments, their breathing,   talking,
laughing,   gesturing,   eating & afterwards
playing on instruments perhaps,   or tense in
conversation
                swept into dancing movement,
in their singing
               They would
fill the rooms & windows,
                     the sky, the few pale clouds
accompanying them   to follow
their doings,
           the sea beginning to
speak a cousin's language
                 (as Danish is to English)
to teach them daring: a half phrase
repeated,
        echo of
ruffled consonants in Danish,
                vowels dropping
& breaking,
         lights of the
midsummer sun unfolding
calmly,
       the shadows fearless.

Wild Oleander

I remember the stony hillside
I wandered on,
                    the rocky slopes,
the stone walls lining the fields
                    & here & there
an extraordinary blossoming, flamy and soft,
of oleander in unplanned corners
of the roads,   bushes grown out of seeds scattered
by the sea-wind,   untended, unprotected
in unforeseeable places.
                    Coming upon them
on that coastline I came upon
love unexpected
                    where the heat
was such it might have withered
all tenderness in the shade of cliffs
the color of lava burning,   where our eyes met and
attempted to turn away, to leave each other, to
close their lids,   shield themselves
from each other,   go into hiding.
                    But the least movement of your arm,
the very shape of my fingers,   even
the politeness in your voice—your hesitation
in saying my name
                    made traitors
of us,   our discretion.
                    August without a single
cloud, not a breath of
rainfall,   no faintest
stirring of wind even
in that cove,   that *cala* where the waves slid forward
again & again with deliberate
fatefulness   again & again   casting
a spell,   weaving a net of spray to
trap us in,   if not the first time,   then
the next,   if not then, the next day.   So even
hearing you in the distance, speaking
to someone else about the weather or
plane-connections could tell me
                         (but tell no one else)
that you were thinking of me
                         (and this was true, you said)
Not even the cliffs I ran along,   the precipice
I clung to the brink of were

more dangerous than our loving.
                            What I risked
going to the edge of them was equal to
our intransigeance.
                        It was danger
sent me out to the rocky hillsides,   the uncertain
pathways,
                    danger sped me
along the stony fields to marvel
at those flowers opening their calyxes
precariously,
                            splendid
because uncared-for,
                            tossed away
so only stones could see them.

Moon-Dust

Tender as Spanish dust & gentle
with whom I walked barefoot
the Mediterranean beaches
                    soft roads
of that white island
                gentle as dust
beneath the mule-drawn wagons
                      or feet
of thoughtful goats led daily by a string in the
                        hand
light-riddled   sky-ridden island
like our love,
                moored to transparencies
rising,   falling
with them   buoyed by the sea & moving
                So I held your body
against my breast
                so we rose & fell with the sea
The ancient watchtower on the beach rose up
to stare at us   & the sliding
constellations
             what stars too leaped surprised
with the fishes out of the sea
                 Our hands
met smiling   the half-shut match-box
sprang out of your fingers
                 "I was frightened
too" you said
           In the cold air
                  afterwards
I held your feet in my hands
                  Moon-white
Ibiza lay
           innocent

Girl Reading a Letter (Vermeer)

The light impinging on space:
                                    I had thought
this would make for wideness
to stride in,
                        an open meadow,
                                            horizon—
a vacant field & the sky immense over gently rolling
hillocks,   or pastures:
an even flatness,
                        but here
                                    there is
light overlapping on
space
        & what happens is
not a flatness,   but its opposite—
a focus where the eye falls deeper
the more it looks,
                        into a
greater depth:
                        a multiple charge,
                        a heat
of concentration,   with everything
pressed together.
                        Let those who speak of
the pleasure of surfaces stand here
                        & look
                        & look,
a million surfaces have shed themselves
into this measure of bliss,
                        this depth.

Lions

These hills swelling,
                    heaving
their flanks toward us
                    are asleep now.
They are lions,   drowsing.
They are sleeping.
                    Once awake
they will astonish us:
                    the strength of
their embraces—their lovemaking
with us who watch them now.
                              They are sure that
the air affirms them,
                    their fullness
in waiting—that promise,
                    more than
an anticipation.   It is the future etched on
the visible, so what will be seems already
to be there,   seems
here.
        I see it also in these trees
without a single new bud,   not a fresh leaf
no twig that's new   but
filled with the light streaming around them & out of them,
                                                        lit

from the inside   from the pith
that the buried root extends to—
                              so curved, so lit-up in
a dance rejoicing.
                    Weather, doubt, fear,
impending coolth and premonition—
all these fall away,
                    so trustful
these branching arms & to be
trusted in,   they tell us
that this present,
                    this moment of April
is what their dance is,
                    what we praise.

No Other Magic

At the end of summer   there is a darkness,
                                        a coolth,
then the air lightens   the warmth
returns,   no longer heavy
                        but lightly
enfolding what it touches: full trees,   voices
                    of young people setting out—
                    those leaves that have been
green now, over months.   It caresses them.
                        The sun holds us: we are in
a suspension—where before this, it ignored us,
                                        bore
down on us blindly   as if to stun,   to
topple.
            Hips, shin-bones, arms, thigh-bones
pressed down on the air   to hold us, keep us
upright.
            Now there is
stillness.
            Everything
spreads wider.
                What I longed for
at 20—that the walls would
fall,   the fences
come down   has begun to
happen.
            Arms' reach,   the eyes ranging—they look for
no other magic:
                They are the poems
which the poem obscures
                        while it is
being written.

Haunted

The last time we were together
after parting
            & I come back to
take my books away
                    an accident
of touch brought back the joy of
nearness under those layers of
                           humiliation,
anger, grief suppressed,
                    flung them
away for refuge
            & us into
each other's bodies
rediscovered: the double wheel—
as if there were no other way to
receiving,   taking wholly from each other
again, again in
absoluteness,
              in our certainty no longer
upright.
        We could see the stars   (ours).
The bridge began to form, but
standing again   we did not dare to
tread on it,
          a wing of fear hung over,
                        a dark bird's wing.
We did not dare to build it.
                  Greyness
covered the sky
          blurring
our eyes.
        Our hands were haunted,
                  until one by one
the stars we had watched
went out.

Untitled

I am a daughter of
the daughters of Jerusalem
                          I am the one who
searched for her beloved by night
                              & found him not
At the gates, in the streets of
the city
        I found him not
                  at
the doorways
I am the one who ran to meet him, ran
                          with my arms outstretched
toward him in '63
             & wept my tears
             with his tears
when illness came to
destroy us,
          to cut us
down
        who ran to meet him two years earlier
in my peasant skirt   when he came down the hill
                back from the continent
to Ibiza
        when we could not
stop our kissing, hugging, smiling, squeezing,
murmuring, could not stop
our joy

Then Another Petal

That last time, Mallorca,
                    as I came on the beach,
                    out of the water
scoured by the sea's salt,
                    warmed
in the sun—how could I have known: this was
the last day,   the end, almost of happiness
                              (having overcome so much)
that only minutes at a time would be left us?
                    The dark message of
your tiredness we could not interpret
                          "Goddess" you said or
something of that sort, half-joking.
                    The end too of the beauty you knew
which drew you to me,
                    glowing then with the color
of sunlight,   cleared   polished
by all the fruits of the sea.
                    All afternoon
we lived in a daze of happiness,
                        that last day
for us of a love unshadowed.
                    We could not see
that the sky,   the sea,   the sun (even)
had turned their faces away.
                    Twenty-four years later,
I watch these wild lilies—delicate curves of
petals, marked with red dashes.
                    Mornings, evenings,
I see the curled petals fall, crescents
furled on the floor.
                    Their scent is fading.
                          The strong
fragrance of a rose, magenta-colored, has
overpowered them—a sweetness unfailing,   splendid
in self-rejoicing
                as I was
that day in August,.'62.
                  But how little
the rose concerns me.
                  It is the wild lily
I watch,   marvelling
at its furling,
                seeing it
drop another,   another,   then
another petal on the floor.

Altamira

Across Spain under that changing
unchanging sky   a new heart made
                          we found
our way to Santillana & the hills
near Altamira & I knew
in the rain   on the oceanfront
at Santander   but poetry
alone will save us
                          & the rain came down
Children scurried through the puddles
                          young couples
clasped each other in the wet
                          lingered
in doorways   Umbrellas
flew open   in the cafes
the Spanish business-men played cards
                          But in the Restaurante
Tipico the faces of the workers
both the old ones & the young were of
untouchable beauty
                          I knew then
that what I knew was nothing
                          Climbing the hills
near Altamira   down again & in the mansion
at Santillana   I knew that this
was not enough.
            The caves
of Altamira badly lit   the silly guide
the tourists   the electric light
                          the rock-
walls the figures on the ceiling—delicate
more than I had thought—the tender feet
the tails the eyes & ears of horses, elephants
and deer   intimate & fresher than the mornings
of last summer in a Mediterranean
landscape set in the new heart   all these
are mute   are nothing
            even from them
I cannot learn
            if we are lost,
                          if we are not
spoken for

IV Give Birth to Yourself He Said

Charlotte's Painting
At The Laundry

Pale 2/3 of a moon over the green leaves,
the air clear and
inside the gallery
                    the exact, the most necessary
red in the perfect place
on the canvas,
                the orange
exactly there,   where it
must be,
            the precise
line & the white erasing
just so much & no more
                        The clear eye of
a child painting what the pulse tells it
to,
        painting outside itself
                            what moves & opens,
closes, withdraws, emerges
inside the body,
                    under
the skin   & with the skin also,
                            waiting
as a child waits
                    & as the persistently
thinking grown-up   can also
wait   for what
cannot be altered,
                    for the unchangeable
most final brush-stroke
                        that makes the canvas
shudder,   makes it climb
into itself,
            that makes it rest.

Haifa

Scooped out of a fiercer morning,   cup
thrust out of rock & desert,
                                    scars
of conflict grooved you,
                            wrenched each bone
in the rib–cage,
                        every vertebra
naked shone through your skin
                            Small city
in the uprisen squareness of
white houses built of the hill
                            Light
plants there the fig & almond squatly
rejoicing
            With hyacinths your promontory
bestrides the sea,
                    from where
all views are equal: purple Syrian hills
and weight of Mediterranean surf
rounding your cup
                    No quiver
stirs the anemone, struck dumb
in scalping light
                    Tension of thorny hill & donkey braying
hardens the breath
                    Hold still,
                                small city,
your cup

That Last Walk

                That last walk
of the winter
                walking
to breathe in alone the white un-
broken snow
                Ice-floes
on the river
                the light behind me
guarding the shadows to walk in their
pride of straightness
                        in the early
evening
            the darkness swept
by the reflections of light
                            Light
off the barges
                boats   the striding
past them
            losing   finding
                        losing
again
            the losing in the muck of winter
that was mine
            of despair
                    What was it
                        brought me
past it?
        Was it a love
brought us?
        Was it?
                    a jungle of
bitternesses?
        of the seldom
touching?

Claire

That she delights in so much,
that she so much delights in
so many things—
                    is delightful
in her
        & the power of wonder
in her
        & that edge of
fierceness
            as I discovered it
many years ago in
the tiger-lily,
                not having
guessed, as a child, that
beauty could be fierce also
& that fierceness itself was
what made the lily flame—
                            those pointed
tendrils,
        deep orange,   the petals
darkly streaked & fiery
enough to burn my mouth, my finger-tips,
the skin between my breasts
                        That a lily could be
fierce & leave its edge of fire
in the air
            not to be extinguished—

For Simone Weil

Would you
        perhaps
write for the poor
           the old
woman who cannot cross the street
                   for weakness
and whose shoes are
misshapen damp rags
            between whom and her life there stands
no screen, no muffling
element
      nothing at all
beyond reality.

        Empty branches
cross the sky in leadings and where
leaves and snow also have fallen
away
    are unburdened!
            they scarcely
move but are always in
motion,
     reaching
tensely to each other for what
they find: not in loneliness but bound together
to themselves
        A severity
not strait nor grey
           except the grey
of light,
     the deeper almost blue
which moves most often
in bending

Your Room

Your room. The big tree outside you
watched changing from wind to
grass to stream: the light that came

through all the windows & green
shadows of bushes moving with
frequent birds. Unexpected

insects shift about in the leaves
speaking noisily, making
the daisies heavy. But we can learn other

wise, other things, when the blinds
are drawn   the light half-seen
your knees become momentous —what we

know, what we discover when the book hints
only   (curve of your ear,   shape of
your eyelids listening

What we do then is what the sea
does!   Enormous

The Exchange

What was golden earlier,
                            an autumn
of sprays shaking their live colors
off the dark branches
                          is a half-lingering
in the air now,   making people stop & wonder
which way to go   what crossing
to take?
             The fruits piled & shining
on the pavement stalls, apples & grapes, bananas,
I pass & store them inside me
                                  & the house-fronts
I'm fond of,   afternoon
light—a warm crystal,   the building-
crane: a tall mobile
in the sky.
                Clouds gather,   making
the light serious,   the streets longer,
a fold of the river turning grey,
                                  a space opening
between the clouds—
                       there only
the light looking back at us
enters into us   becoming
an exchange of eyes.

Elegy for Dylan Thomas

Suddenly that
voice as it had been
living spoke and we looked
at each other dying
into his life
           drowned
by the salt of the green-tide rising
from toes' root and nails
of flesh and the mushroom tremor
of tongue and that breaking forth

Which flush
in the cold sky apricot
bird noises coming out after rain
that redness
the rhododendron breaking
kingly from the brown pod in June in
setting of domed crowns open on to
branches and splendor given
from the dry sporangia to the always
now the always ending summer

The Leaf

I was happy that reason tapers
as a tower above the sea.
                        Adrian Stokes

Southward
            and the first warm breath
            the first Italian
roofs & streets
                  a courtyard
with a fountain
                        windows open
in the evenings,
                        exact in tenderness
the balances
            the fronts of houses
stairs mouldings
on the arches
                  infusing
deeply a peace
                  Already the Mediterranean
in those hills stood cupped & waiting
Centuries offered their hands to us
firmly shaped,
                  fountains
welcoming in garden squares
in Bellinzona
                  We moved southwards
to Rome   Naples   then to the east
and middle orient where my father
gentle & thin   his body
hot & quiet   lay dying
                        I think of my father
with the innocent eyes
                  I see him
tossed across Europe in a tide of youth
westward through Germany
                        from Riga
to the Swiss cities & America
                        drawn
by a dream of brotherhood
                              bewildered
by much he saw,
                  longing
for some wider ease,
                  some richness,
                        deeply

in the edged world
                    lost & floating,
smiling,
        then sadly,   like a leaf
                            Now
on the high tide of his dying
                        rose outstretched
and fell
struggling for breath
                    (With our look
                    we pierced the heart of
                    that secret by which man makes himself
                    out of what reflects him, there
                    in Venice—so that the elements,
                    once hostile, are made
                    loving—dense on the track of
                    a mystery of reflection,
                                        stepping
                    in the enormous traces of dreams,
                    the half-remembered
                                        So
                    touching Venice
                    does one touch the magic of
                    one's own particular
                    good fortune)
                            Over us
                    the three lucky horses tossed their manes
                    and snorted
                    gold
It was the next hot day
                    (in Florence
my father died
            The fever rose
steadily   Nothing
could check it
        Up the bell-tower
        I staggered
                    in the noonday
                    heat
                    Through the wall-slits the city
        swam in a glare
                    The chapel
        moved in its points & massed them
        (stars in their constellations)
                                        the eternal
        clock
                    Only his heart stopped then
        & he was dead. That evening in the

close heat & the next day,
                            passing
the hill-towns secret as mediæval
manuscripts,
                    we did not know him
dead
        Neither in the Roman
Forum
            where the starved kitten
wailed,   nor overlooking
the Tiber
                nor in Pompei,
nor Sorrento
                    Those stones & arches only
                    said: Here
In a summer of Mediterranean brilliance
he grew colder
                    & more lost,
was gently gone away
without a look
                    except for the last
gesture: two summers earlier
slow eyes watching from a distance
behind the face
Pity the old
        for they are no longer
sure of how they move
or if they properly
can see or hear you
                        but they can remember
                        how it was otherwise
Out of such heavy heat
into the cold & dark
the shrunken body in the burial cloth,
                            who once
sat brooding Kabbalistic mysteries
            High in the hills
of Galilee we saw the town
settled by Kabbalists
                    (where he had never been
a mediæval town in gulfs
                    of space
buoyed up in circles,
sea swimming in light
                    (light thinner still
than the light of Jerusalem:
                    to walk there is
to walk in the sky partly,   but weighted by mountains

                              dense with memory
                              in explicit
thoughtfulness
And the end of pity is not a grief,
                                        but a change
(Here in Germany,
                    where so many of my kin
                    or kin's kin were coldly done to death
& the spring dares to come again in the squirrel's shape,
we can hope
              together with the bluejay
              they will transform it)

In spite of my ancient longing
for the gods & priestesses of the Carmel
and the sea & for the Cretan who, September,
shook our boat
                in the Mediterranean,
                                        darkened
the summer air
                let me give praise
                to the intelligence which cherishes
                & knows,
                          gathering
                in warm light what the fingers
                of night discover,
                giving tongue
                to all darknesses
                              and praise
                the senses
                          through their power
                          is the intelligence
                          made warm
Other darknesses,
                  confusions
of youth, lostness,
                    (where today walls, stones, houses
                    are the same,
                                  only the faces
                                  new,
                                  the voices)
must be made over,
                    even the unbearable
restored to a true center
                          The veins in the leaf irradiate
their own design: the light behind them
is heat,   is joy

Darknesses
of the nerves' struggling
                    (the body fighting
                    its own death)
as they turn to earth
                    are penetrated
by what we cannot recognize—
                         light & dark transforming
                         what they find,
                         becoming it
That body, nerves & bones & flesh,
                         fallen
into coldness, extremity of cold,
                         lays bare for us
the fire that keeps us warm.

The Slipmoon

One out of every six of the leaves
                         of the cherry
is yellow:
              such a blossoming
of goldfish
                or lemon–quick
or a crocus
              firstly opened;
                              or perhaps
some extraordinary
golden humming-bird

springlike as the slipmoon
this withering

At the Concert

Next to me
            How the light
shone through you
                    Shadows
leapt inside you
                I thought you were made of
the thinnest fruitwood
                        honed
to transparency
                or of the maplewood they use to
shape the great violins of Cremona,
                                    curving
to a vibration,
                their varnish mixed of aloe
with Oriental herbs—a blend discovered,
irreplaceable,   300 years ago

                        What moved
inside your body?
                    Pulses of fire,
of shadow—
            What shook you
in the gusts that fire makes?
                            Your legs,
your arms,   your fingers
                        What lit your eyes
and in your hair?
                What lifted
your breastbone?
                    My hands reaching toward
without choosing,
                without knowledge of you there

Stop   Look Listen

Stop   hold still. You're
alone in the center
of the world. There's a ticking in
your head
              but it will stop also
soon
          There's a swirl
around your body
                          but give it a little
time
          It will settle.

Hold still   Let your
breath come slowly   Let be

The weight around you
turns into clouds or stars   Ease it
Stretch out your eyestrings   Observe
Look   Look
              Look where the everything
grows and leaps up
heaping itself into more   Let the eye then, eye
take, take everything
it can. Never give over.
Pull the world inside   Wedge it
against your space   Fill out
the crevices   Shine back at
it—the world
                  Look
look again   Make your look
bolder   Again
O listen   again. A still-
ness. A circle. You break it where it
pivots you   sliding of the air
in reverse   a movement
at the bottom becoming
the top   You're shifted so that
the weight of your heartbeat
tilts and veers.   Let the sky
run round   Let it shift and outdo itself,
the hinge of the body
splinter   (the iron
cry out
          Your ears
indented
              Ride out then
through the fuller
season

Tide

Under the pine-trees
pine-needles
           the blue jays
call loudly
          The mat of pine-cones
has a heavy smell
        I wade in puddles
of sunlight where before it was
shadowy
between the branches

          There are taller
lights among the trees now
         The bird-cries
are more questioning

        I wished you there
your brown neck
in the sunlight   those birds
in rapid conversation
over us   the fall of your hair.
          What turn
now?
        What shift into
            (a bewilderment
the waters gathering to their full
           as the moon,
the moon draws them,
          contracts
and widens
       Through this hole
now in the universe
         this (pain
unexpected   These currents.

Will the moon-curve
balance them
        in its further
reckoning?
        Will the light
            intaken
take refuge again in those eyes
exhaling
      a darkness

Candles

for Stanley Kunitz

It is the silence which surrounds them that makes me
peaceful,   a depth
around them:
            when I come upon them,
                                    forgetting
they are there,   lit-up & pointing
upwards
            as if they were
praying.
            It is their steadiness—
especially the smaller of them which
burn gravely,
                  are more full
                              Only
the tall ones seem to
be endangered—having ventured
so far, so high—
                  danger
can find them easily.
                  They are open
to the winds that buffet them.
                              Even
their own breathing can become uncertain,
                                    causing them
to waver,
            their own heartbeat
fitful, strenuous,
                  a fever
of longing,
            sometimes even
a longing to go backward,
                              falter,
to give up whatever they were
made for:
            that persisting.
But how short their moment
of despairing:
                  space deepens
around them,
            for the shape of
their continuing is faithful,
                              a sweeping,
                              a stretching out of

distance in tenderness.
                        It is not
a single word that they are saying
over & over,
                    not a salutation,
not even a blessing.
                        It is that all languages
are fused together here,
                        breathed out
in this light & forgotten.
                        The body
rising from its sleep, out of
the caves of its own darkness is given
its height in continuance,
                            the wick blown upon,
the tip shaken,   light uneven.
                        Silence dug out
deeper than a tree-root,
                        so deep there is
no word yet, only a
fragrance.
            Something is guarded—
neither evening nor morning
                            Something watched over here,
but not a phrase yet, not a syllable.

As If for the First Time

for Eugene Morley

Years of looking at
that photograph
    & only yesterday
I saw them: the hooded
figures, (heads bent slightly
forward, cowled, against the harp-shape,
       shape of an organ)
     shadows
emanating heat, not coldness,
        banked fires
in that photograph (your stage-set)
       They were
yourself—your guarded fire,
      (hooded & cowled)
      emerging
in sparks & flashes, or in flames
smouldering,
   but never
the full blaze.
     That day of seeing was of
spring in January
     Suddenly
the mild air, the sky alight, the unforeseen occurring
daily, visibly (for weeks before)
       Dry leaves
shaken off,
    upheavals
of the smaller roots,
      trembling
of branches, their unclenching.
       The air
shifted.
  Was it here
some brittle twigs might
green themselves? I wondered
      Was it
a new breath?
    That dancing
of energies in flight over
the grey pavements,
     swelling
of the smallest leaves
    & later
in the intermittencies of

rain-drizzle,
                little voices
trying their own notes out
for the first time,   essaying
language—
            the birds.
                        If those cowled heads are language
(in the photograph)   those gestures
tied to gravity—if they are words,
                                what you meant
to say,   whatever you were   was
still half-spoken when
you died.
            Lightness
of your movements too rooted in
the rocks you stood on,   laughter
veiled,
            a radiance
broken into fragments,   each new beginning
rimmed by a doom,   each morning
tied too closely to the dark.
                            But that the season, the year
begins again: the outgoing,   the incoming
of the tide continues hugely as before,
                                the waters
swelling on its surface   as leaves, branches sprouting,
tendrils,   wings making motions
half-learned or never learned
before swim with it   Let us
try the unforeseeable—everything
as if the first time—

our own.

Eye-Chant

for Claire Moore: her drawing

Eye of the storm
                    you might have
been
        who are
an eye of the blue sun,
                            the greener
eye of a moving hillside,
                            who are the eye of the half-
                                            moon
covering another sun,
broken,
            who are the needle's
eye,
        splitting the dark side
of the moon which breathes into
a sun,
            who are the eye
of the heat,
                eye of the heart's
nerve, eye of the knowing
glance,
            the look which does not
waver when it moves
                        You are the eye
of the light & of the dark which follows
it,
        eye of the inside world   burning
from green to blue
                        & of the outside, back to
green & darker
green
            (out of a darkness into
            a stretch of breathing)
eye of my inside ocean & of
the outside valleys
tumbling
greening

Weather

That odor,
          late January,
of a spring coming
too early
              was enough to
arouse the birds.
                  Was it a delusion when
they set out chirping: Faith Hope & Love?
The weather seemed certain—
it was undeniable
                  I flew with them,
basked as they did in
that amazing warmth
                    I spread wings also

What changeableness
of weather,   what
shifting from warm to cold,
                          what varying
of the wind's direction
                    what of
mutability
other than my own sign, my constellation, can I
find to hold responsible
for this untowardness:
                      the solstice cracking
open—who should be
weather-wiser,
                toughened to forty
springs in January,
steadier in the southwest wind than I am,
as I am not

No Word

the language
              is not   does not
have words for
                   unknown (known)
                   the not known
that is known
              as the stone might
deny   in saying what would
wish to be denied,
                   what has not
said   what cannot
be spoken,   be written,
                   heard,
heard
              Can the stone
read   write   itself
                   & the eyes
we did not   could not
meet
              What was seen: no word
                                   (Celan
       & swearing
to remember
                   only the barbed-wire
fence
       the electric charge remembers
the child's face,   3 years old,
                            holding
her grandfather's hand
                   my face
it was   my eyes at 3
                   & she frightened
of what was more than
                   more than
to be frightened of,
                   no words
the white body of the 20-year old,
dark hair, queenly
head, breasts of a
goddess,   flung onto
the pile of corpses,   holding
her cousin's hand,
                   not spoken
                   not to be said

the older woman,
                    face of an older
Nefertete   the eyes have seen
                        cannot speak it
cannot be said
                the old man
with the face of a prophet,
                            beaten
to the ground

The Hawk

                    Cactus-wren
in the desert,   barely
a voice,   low, low,   continual,
                                        more
delicate than any fluting,
                                persistent
as the sound of water would be,
                                    if there were
water   here where everything
thrives with no sign of it
                        No trace here of
man's soiling or
man's rubbish.
                    The blossoming plants
have leaves here that are
cut boldly.
                Silence should have
a different name here,
                            nor is
stillness the name for it.
                            We are held up in it
by enormous wings.
                            They are made out of
light,   made of transparency,
of the sky
                to which the earth is
joined,
            for the hawk sees us
with indifference
                            flying past us
for which we can be grateful.
                            The hawk
joins them.

Summer Still

I look around
                    & it is
summer, summer still,
                 August—
time still for the sun to reach us,
for us to lie together in
the sun's eye,   dozing
                   (obliterating
                   all the moons
                   we missed
          All summer
there has been a profusion
of leaves,   much heat,   much dampness
                        & under
the old leaves,   new ones
pointing upwards   half-hidden & beginning
to burst open
                 & alongside the new leaves
intimations of still smaller
beginnings
              barely defined & not yet measurable
in inches,
            in lengths & swellings known only
to vegetables,
              the roots of them
in darkness—
             an inwardness
stretched out invisibly,   their searching
a direction
            We've lived in a plant-country,
immensely thick—a denseness
of dark-green hanging
over us
         & yesterday I saw the foliage
in a million possibilities of leaves, branches, joined together
in half-darkness,   early evening—the park
                    & it is light,
light's action joining them
           Such a summer—
such heat & denseness—
               never
have I known a summer like it
                 If there are
so many leaves—the differing shapes,

green variegated growing one near the other,
                                        think how many
more can still grow,
                    what other greenness,
                                        never
the same exactly,
                    never shapeliness
repeated,
            think how many days there are, how much
weather,
            what clusters of
half-thoughts,
                    musings
warm as touching,
                        gathering
of life's heat now
                        the end of summer,
now this turning   a full curve,
                                a wave unfurling,
leaning over of the season into
the greater cool
                & the stem of it
deeper,
        where roots push down into
a darkness

Salisbury

           Entering
through that arch into
the garden of the canonry
                 & beyond it—
the other garden along the river,
                  tall rows of
flowers: hollyhocks, delphinium, nasturtium,
               bushes
of white bellflowers,
           beyond them
the heavy-laden willow-trees,   the river
             & 2 boys fishing

On the river's far side fat brown-and-white
cows are grazing (Constable
            Slowly,
no matter how slowly I walk, it's too fast for
this place,   too hasty,
           too superficial,
for everything is rooted here more than
we believed it could be:
           there's no reason
to leave it, ever.
           And stepping's allowed only
as another kind of standing,
           another
stillness,
      another way of
being rooted,
         of growing beneficent
& sunlit,
        connected
with each leaf, each twig, petal or
blade,
      no more, no less than
they,
   having got beyond
grieving

Two Reds

Two reds there are:
                           strawberries
and strawberry leaves
                            on the brown earth
among the green weeds
                          where I
crouch
       searching for them
hot in the sun
                  to see cleanly
the blob of red,
               sharp
center of vulnerability!
                      delicate
on the tongue and eyeball where the sun
burns through the leaf
                not the berry.
                I stoop over
leaning on the red drop;
                 heart's
brightness deeply set there
                   where the sun burned through it
left an iron tongue.
              The reds
are different
            and the cardinal
                    crimson—
cool as tulips
            bluely in the clear air
shows a lipped sweetness
                 Scarlet
a tropical fruit
            the tanager
whose black tuft crests
            a furious eye
and tailing indignation
                What redness cool or fiery,
                      burning
transparency or glancing
dark
    in wetness issuing
upon the tongue
            with fire
inside!
       are undissolved

either in heat or light
                    consumed as color
is, by fire
         in sweetness

The Long Curve

The spray on both headlands
dashed against rocks in
resolution
          is
fate:
      a finality in the abandon—
                            foam
lifted higher than possible into
a moment's crown,
                a destiny
completed.
         From this distance
there is nothing but
absolute disappearance—a shattering—
except ending,
            but watching
the shape of it (again)
                  splashing
into the headland,   trying
the impossible: to wipe out what might be
harder than itself,   reaching
finally an acceptance—
                  the long curve of it
could begin to
signify a returning,
             a coming home.

The Clouds Stretch Out

                        Looking across into
the space of winter changing into
a depth
            beyond the line of little
boats and launches,
                        their masts hopeful
in the breeze, alive,
                        the clouds stretch out
greyer than water, but unerring
in a flight of speeds
mastering the lights above the branches
                        where the leaves have
turned, turned, crackle
in the grass, you can tread on them

            My body
is tall and silent now in a long
dark coat, enclosed in itself, inside a hollow
tree-trunk walking:
                        the lights are changing.
                        Walk farther now into another
afternoon;
            the sky is swifter, but not a single
light is relinquished, not a color, not a
direction
            How much one can walk now and even
later (even later)
                        Nothing is over,
                                    Only a further depth
reflected

The Flute

In a human wasteland
the courtyard here
                        Westbeth
early
        notes of a flute,
the morning innocent still
of any noise
                        Now the thoughtful
phrases breathed & ribboned out
in curves,
            purity
of sound for its own sake,
                                its being
sound only
                    The flute spilling
itself outward,   rippling,
funnelling itself into
clarity of intention,
                        into beginning,
completion.

Hamlet Act I Scene I

Who's there?
             (so it begins)
Nay, answer me;
                stand & unfold
                yourself
So it begins
             & we stand challenged.
                              Unfold
& open yourself for what you are,
                        undo the doors
of your disguises.
                Expose the core-like
workings: methods
of your concealments
                (oil the hinges)
                        and answer:
Time for delay there is none.
                     Push aside
layer after farther layer of
sliding barriers.
             Time presses.
Danger.
        Stand & answer
now.
        Who's there?
                    is there?
                        You standing
unfolding
        with your piece by piece
map,
     where each
     barrier
folds away into
itself
        & where the world is a circle
imprinted by the globe.
                     The curtains
drawn back
             & inside it
the inner & the outer theater:
                        a heaven
above, the earth below,
                     yourself an axis
among the stars,
             the universe reflecting
itself,
        yourself
reflected.

For Federico Garcia Lorca

For years now,
             I have been
eating your death, Federico
a heavy substance,
                        medicine
that I must take.
                  For years it has been
on the edge of my plate
                    & I have tasted it,
a mouthful at a time,
                    turning my head away
at times, spitting some of it back.
                            I have not wished
to see it—
        the slightest savor of it
was more than enough.
                    I turned my head away
& pushed away the plate,
                    refusing it.
For 2 years now,   I have begun to
sip at it,
        small mouthful by
mouthful:
        a dark substance
spreading a stain in my blood
                            2 years now.
                            3 weeks ago I saw
the moon of your country
                    hanging
over the Vega,
            holding still in
the sky:
        pale yellow & growing yellower—
witness to your childhood,
youth,   your impossible death.
                        There was
no smiling in it—
only a memory of a sweetness,
                        a waiting
to testify,
        a wide grief,
a patience—
        a pale honeycomb which may be filled again
with honey,

                  awaiting its time,
                                    needing no answer
from us, watchful, abiding.
                              Pale golden, the bees return
from the early mimosa,
                          the wild iris of the Alhambra hill,
the hidden crocus,
                      the honeysuckle.
The moon is filled with their humming.
In flight after flight they bring back with them
their gold,
                  to fill up your paleness, moon,
heap up the weight of your witnessing,
burnish it,
                  ponderous
as bronze,   a brazen shield,
                                    the moon that watched over
your birth, Federico,   your growing,
                              that stood by helpless,
unable to make a sound when they killed you.
                          While here in another country
the moon is a monosyllable
                              precisely spoken
in Italian,   distinctly edged
in eloquence as a hill,   a terrace,
                                    a finality
commanding recognition,
                              perfectly arched
& clear,
            asserting grace.

Curve of the Water

To make that curve of the water
live— to make it so,   extended
into space wholly its own
                              & the rocks
part of the curve & therefore
grown into the hillside
                      .   & where the water is
green unexpectedly,
                    it is
the source of all other greens,
                              it is
of a green not leaf—   not moss-green,
                                        not even
green of the bracken   but contains them: is
the well out of which they come,   to which they also
return—is their harbor.
                        The flame-oranges,
the reds, dark fires,
                    the burnt-out
red sienas,   thinned out yellow mirrors
of each other,
              they flare up now
out of whatever is,   even on
the blue water   the blueness of it.
                              They are there to
be the not-expected,
                    what is at variance to
what we know.
            We see them but
they are not held as seen, not kept there
behind the eyes,   never wholly
remembered,
            as if a bird's wing had
flashed sideways
                in the sunlight
to prove us earthbound
                      (our slowness
itself impossible
to hold.

Weight & Lightness

If at first the kissing
of each other's hands seemed
only affection,   only tenderness,   holding
of the other's hand tightly   (with both hands)
                              or stroking
of the hair, nape of the neck
                              & even
leaning of heads toward
each other
             followed by
a shyness, the eyes cast down marvelling
What has happened?   What can be
happening?   What is this?
                              So the eyes brush
each other again—it is
with another knowledge curtaining
the eyelids, breath coming
unevenly,   hands uncertain
of how, where, touch might be
welcomed.   Is it the time?   Is this
the time?   Has time brought us
to this (now)?   Is it now? The time
for us?
          So only to
fall upon each other's shoulders, press
cheeks & lips together,   hold each other
closely,   eyes closing in
half-fear, half-marvelling
                              O,   O, all that the lips
form,   O, the sweetness flowing
through the smooth skin,
                              blood rising
to the surface,   caught breath
weight & lightness leaning
upon the other,   joined, taken
& given back,
                 the low gasps coming
out of earth's sadness dispersed now
in a kind of song,
                    a kind of singing
                    words muffled into
a low humming,   curves
interlocking,   soaring,   holding
to each other,   rages
washed away in a twinning & everything
exhaled together &
                    at once.

Made Out of Links

Your weight sweetly upon me
filling each dip, drop, slope,
                          fitting
each joint, ridge & hillock of
my body's landscape,
                  shoulders finding
the other half,
              heads pressed into
each other,   hands curving along the lengthened
smooth places,
              a shape made out of
links, elongated
beyond our sizes   but forming
a circle:
          how excellently
matched those nearnesses,
                        how well & sweetly
fitted
        those weights, those lightnesses
borne down upon me

The Macaw

   The philosophers say we know nothing
of endlessness, infinity,
         that we cannot
conceive it.
     But mostly our lives
are lived as if we were
infinite, as if there were no
ending.
    Do animals know that the span of
their living is limited?
         Is it
in the eyes of birds, in their quickness,
in the fierceness of their pecking?
          In the fury
of the macaw's beak, his glaring
in the evening? Is this the cause of
his anger?
     How little we know,
          how slowly
whatever we know emerges from
clenched-back beginnings, tightened buds
inside us,
    any kind of
untoward weather, unlikely wind, frost, chill
can keep them closed,
       how many they are,
       how tiny
every beginning inside us
in a darkness.
     Slowly—years
it can take for one or two to push up on
longer stems, make larger petals,
        leaves,
perhaps to open, unfold, encourage others
barely begun, to reach up
after them
     O we are
not finished for so long,
       so much is left there
to sprout, make leaves in a notion
of time without end, forgetting, as if one could
live in the timeless.
      Suddenly, as if from
a bend in the road, we are cut short,
        we are reminded,

time turns on us.
    Our jaws set in fierceness,
          our eyes aware of
danger in the movement of time itself,
        aware of
everything, at once,
     our eyes glare out
into the evening.

Fire-Sign

for S. G.

Lovely
>   O fire of
my heart,
>   you've come up
again,
>   warming
my space,
>   as those logs have
finally caught,
>   leaning
on each other,
>   as fire catches
one spark from another
>   setting in movement
radiance of waves,
>   stored sunlight,
heat that flickers,
>   a curled edge
>   of the air that
has wings,   that wavers
& flies
>   & offers
itself to a winter of seventeen years,
>   these cold stone floors
a warmth that
whirls & scatters:
>   flung light.

Hydrangea

If you should say "Hydrangea"
                        I'm there again,
                                        outside
the hospital,   outskirts of Tel-Aviv
in December
                and breathe in
the green & flowering plantings there
                                with
a kind of terror
                for my mother lies
dying inside
                That is all I can
know or be aware of
                        That & the purply blue cones
of hydrangea   lifting in fullness,
climbing into abundance
                        The hydrangeas,
their smell,   I breathing them in
knowing that they do not matter
at that moment,   that her knowledge
of death approaching,   of pain & fear are
all that is left of the long years of
her living
            & of my wrestling
with her image—that not-knowing, not-being-
understood—now beginning to see her,
                                beginning
to set her where at last I could offer
pride as her daughter
                        to find in her ageing finally
compassion, acceptance,
                        to be nothing else
in those hours,
                nothing else but that: daughter,
what she had sought & longed for blindly
my love

From Outer Space

Moving & delicate
                  we saw you
that time, fragile as a raindrop
                         you seemed then
shining & vulnerable,   in colors
we had not known to be yours,
                           rare, jewel-like,
but more alive than a jewel,
                     grained & printed,
scratched by the finger-nails of living,
                        a thousand
ways of life, millions, even,
                   with that first
lifting of man's foot, heavy on
the surface of the stony moon-rock   we saw you,
for the first time, earth, our earth, young,
fresh, bestowed on us as new,   newest of
all possible new stars,   even knowing you
stained, soiled & trampled
                by our filth,
all of it transmuted somehow into living sapphire,
emerald breathing,   topaz, carnelian, alight with
fire
       Where is our tenderness enough to
care for you?
            O small bell,   lit with living,
swinging into danger!

5 Men in Their 90s on a Rickety Porch in the Appalachians

(a Life photograph)

The hilarity of the old who,   in spite of
everything, laugh—laugh into
the wind of time,   toothless,
                                    with bare gums,
their faces—skin & bones merely,
                                    bald heads, bodies
skeletal,   fingers bony almost
as Yorick's
            (Alas, poor Yorick)
            now at this point
nothing can stop them—
                        nothing
dismay or make them less—
                        diminish
the life that is in them
                        (you looked forward once
                        to being like them—
                        taking part in such gaiety)
crystalline as a stream falling
in silver:
            the summing-up
of everything coming before it—
                                    intense as
mountain air in their laughter,
                        pealing thinly,
stroke after pointed stroke
                        (bells high up in a tower)
clear as pebbles
in icy Alpine water

Survivors

Out of the bare, dried-up
twig of a tree standing
on 26th Street,
                    east side of 8th Avenue
9 huge flowers are blossoming
in rose & lavender:
                    balloons
for a festival this street
could do with,
                    needs—
They are survivors of the snows,
                                        the rains,
the sleet, the icy winter
storms,
            dancing in hardiness
over the heads of people passing,
the ordinary pavements,
                            the dirty, slightly tawdry
streets,
            signs of small businesses,
                                        electric
lights—folk-patterns
of a careless city.
                    4 rosy globes
                    5 lavender ones
flown there with the hopes of New Year's Eve
9 gallant moons

bobbing there,
            dauntless

The Rondanini Pietá

His face seems blinded
with pain
                    & dazed into
anonymity,
                    but she—
woman-mother-beloved & loving
is giving birth to him still,
                                        he issues (still)
from her body,
                    they are
of the same flesh,
                              pressed
together
          & only her touch,
the complete giving,
                              the flow of
her body into his can heal him
                                        She knows that
& dimly, in his pain,
                              he knows it
also,
          as the earth,
          with its leaves,
          its streams
its branches, might
heal a deer
that has been wounded,
                    so she, the mother,
                    pours forth all the power of
her life-streams
                    into him,
seems to warm him,
                              to melt, in
the heat of compassion
                              what is
wounded in him,
                    to take to
herself the pain,
                    to dissolve & become
one with it,
          hide it inside herself,
fill her own flesh with it
                    & perhaps, taking it into herself
change it,
          as branches

filled with a storm can
make a space that is
windless
            beneath them.

Every 3 Days

Every 3 days a storm,
                     but I no longer
feel hilarity at this
cycle,   as I did once
                     The pleasure
I take in it now has to do with
the yellowness,
                     an unresting
half-transparency,
                     light falling,
falling,
          the excitement—all
those storms outside—
                     weather
making a counter-pendulum
swinging against an irregular
inside weather,
                     an intermittency
I should be responsible for,
                     clanging of
bells struck at random,
                     now close, now
distantly
          & I'm thrown past
their clangor
          as I was shaken
by your suffering
                     & then brought past it
by your courage.

Life Returning

There you were,
              & it was
over 9 years since I'd seen you
alive,
          but you were indubitably
there in Mahler's 2nd,   the very words were
the words I'd heard you use in talking
to me: "wings"
                  & "not lived
in vain"
          & "everything
wished for will come"   those words & the music too
so kin to your music with that insistence,
                                      that stillness,
the sudden thrusts,   the pain suppressed
& altered into dance,
                      the underlying
song
          & I saw you too where
the vultures swooped in a ravine over
dead bodies of young men & women   tortured
for their love of freedom
                          & in the faces
of the fishermen's wives in India when they took over
the selling of the catch & in the pride of
their smiling under those ornate headdresses
                                      to celebrate
the new hope in their lives
                          & most of all
the dancing at the festival of the good
triumphing over evil,   in that other Indian village of
the bagpipe player overcome with
joy, the women with transparent veils floating,
                                      the beating
of the drums
              & in the eyes of the little child,
life returning to him,
                  gleaming

Those Two Fires

What do you mean then?
say it.
         Say all of it: what you mean
Say it out now
               (Who am I?)
I am the one in that picture   aged 3,
                                    looking up at
her mother, questioning:
                         (wondering)
that great bulk of a mother as
she seemed to me then
                       (so small a woman as she was)
But what I sense is
her not-quite-thereness for me
                               something
distracted,
           something half-turned away
           & uncertain
of herself & what she should do,
                                 should be
for me or for herself is it?
                         Or for him my father?
Who sits at the beach beside me—how beautiful
                          he is,   thoughtful,
a little overwhelming,
                       but I am delighted
beside him,   to be that
small, that slim female thing,
                               slimmer
than the round-faced child in a
red plaid dress which I still remember,
                                   smiling,
pleased with herself & the doll she's holding,
                                        a doll as
sweet as an angel, surprised at
being held,   astonished
at the touch of a mortal, dazed at
being on earth.
               I am that & that & that one—
the frightened, sad little girl of 7
                              & the other one
pleased at her flowered ample 18th century skirt
               & then there is
one in profile, singing
in a group, learning to follow

sound.
        Who was it, which one remembered
words, words, working like a spell, magic,
                       the magic of
a word: something saying: the wind,
                 something
like "Death can be blown away"
             even
without knowing clearly what death was,
what was meant.
        So much was
        difficult, so much before what was easy,
                      then

difficult again,   seeming
to be much admired,
          to be
loved,   but groping,
         barely
sure of anything but a single step,
             the future
always misted,   always with
darkness in it.
        Those two fires—fire of
the eyes looking,
        of the body's knowledge,
so long in moving together
           difficult & slow in
meeting.

Behind the Cellar-Door

20 times at least   I remember
to have died & been born again—
                                again
thrown back to the dark places,
                        deep in
the underground,
                undergoing
darkness,   flung apart there,
undone,
            to come together again
                        (Osiris-like)
rise again,
            grains of darkness
on my heels,   soil
streaking my body,
                        clods of earth on
the palms of my hands
                        that helped me
                        climbing
out of shadow:
                What bulb sunk in the earth can
come to its birth & open again,
                        scattering
deep smells of moisture,
                        dirt sticking
to it,
        finding new air or making
air new   as we can?
                    Behind the cellar-door
the floor is coming
apart,
        green blades stick up through the cracks,
                                breaking
the form,
            damp flooring smells,
cement rotting & a rankness
of grass-blades & roots spatter
the air.   .
            How many richnesses
can unfold still?
                So the center be unfingered
                the depth unbroken.

Esteban's Drawing

What's held
along the edges & the center
                              where everything
is bound & not one
breath escapes in breaking,
                              is
filled & known,
                all contours nourished, not a single
bone deprived.
                So nothing falls apart here
in this world of falling
where all tilts & is about to fall.
                                    There is no
need for plucking out the heart,
                              no need to
grope here where the eye is
seriously alive—
                Because the black, the grey, the white
                              & lesser
greys mysteriously move in varied centers
of displacement,
                your drawing, Esteban Vicente,
has made me happy.

Curious Flower

"I eternally see her figure
eternally vanishing"
                              Keats did not
want to die
                    and was in misery.
                         For Baudelaire often
the weight of guilt was equal almost
to death
                    They tipped the balance
level.
              But those dying
in the ghetto
cried   Do not forget us but do not
weep for it will not help

Some others
about to die were strangely
quiet and as if filled with
gratitude & knowledge
                              They loved
the earth   but a light surrounded
them. It was for them to speak in
consolation to offer
wisdom   a curious
flower,
              disclosing all its fullness
in pride
the day before its death only

For W. C. Williams

In all the deepest thrusting
points of my knowledge
                        bearing
the weight on them of
                        those sharpest moments on which
everything depended—
                    there you spoke (them
words jutting out of
those crevices bursting
                        open where the center is: there
It was said,   as I have longed to
say it,   do it
                & continue
from there,   from the hundreds of
theres   leading
into tangents
                which when
you speak them,   cease to
be tangents: are center
                        And the breaks,
                        the pauses,
parentheses, diminuendos,
                        accelerandos
                            you have dared
accomplish them
                & I tremble over them in fierceness
of recognition
                now I have found you at last
                            whose hand I can
take in trustfulness
                closest of
those who have fathered me, whom
                            in your lifetime
I did not come to see,   out of
diffidence that has cursed & almost damned me
With what certainty you say your say—as I would
write those words on the skin of
my body—tattoo my chest with them,   so
I said at dinner less than
3 nights ago
                I rise to
your bait,
            I am your fish
                        swimming
in the darkest waters of

our time,
        in this wastage,
this ugliness,
            corruption
of our cities,
            blurring of
distinctions,
            breakdown of
language as of everything for which there must be
ears   to listen to more than
poundings only,
                eyes to see
more than gloss, shine, glitter
                        to see
sharply
        & behind things
                    To your word
I rise up saying "thoughts alight & scatter"
                            They begin!
"the perfections are sharpened"
                        I bow to you,
I, like you, having
            "only of late, late!
begun to know, to
know clearly (as through clear ice)
                        whence I draw my breath
or how to employ it clearly—if not well—"
                            Hearing today in
this Elizabethan garden in Oxfordshire
                    the strong clarity
of bird-speech
            as you heard
"the red-breast . . . clearly!"
                    the harsh song of
the Icterine Warbler recalling
                "both the Nightingale's and
                the Marsh Warbler's" song,
though "the jumble of notes each repeated . . . includes both
musical and discordant ones",
                    it rings out
in defiance, a ring of energy pitted
against the world,
            the late, green-leaved,
half-greening, half-wet, sometimes shining
world
        Rising, I bow to you,   searcher,
dealer in truth,   refusing

"the non-purveyors"
                              refusing
to pretend direction. Whither? I
cannot say, I cannot say
more than now . . . watching—
colder than stone.
                              alone
in a wind that does not move the others—
                                             knowing
"There is no recurrence. The past is dead."
I climb in the tracks you made,
                              in your despair,
humility—where you split the rocks & tore them
with your fingers,
                              where your hands were torn
open.
            With what certainty
                              & despite
the "divisions . . . imbalances" despite "the vague.
the particular no less vague" the knowledge of
"terrible things"
                  with what certainty
you say your say
                  though "there has been again & again
a terrible postponement"
                              Barely clinging
to the edge of a plank,
                              dragged on my knees
in the wake of an iron chariot,   I knew
the numbed attempts at speech,
                              blind efforts
of touching,   the inarticulate cries, the brushing past of
voices, the deaf singing, years of spasmodic
scribbling,
            but warmed by your brooding fire,
                                             made over
by your patience,   impatience,   despair,
                                             with
nothing lost, nothing left-out,
                              nothing
uncared for.
            True father of my spirit
I acknowledge you,
                  my joy in you
public & secret both—knowing what must be
torn away, dislodged, pulled down,
                              so invention

can begin.
        Later than most I come
to you,
       & needing to expiate
the tardiness, as all my other tardinesses in
self-awareness.
          Streams, water, the loosing
of tides & currents,
            winds shaping
the surface of water into differing
crests,   the drive & texture
of waves,
        have held me, as
they have given you images of
the movements of gathering thoughts or
thought scattered
          For me, more often
standing at the edge of the sea, watching
what moves stealthily off the horizon
              & deeply, invisibly
almost begins a slow stride, a dance in
several directions at once
          for me the sea is
catharsis, a scouring, a stripping away of extraneous elements
a cleansing,   a rebirth.
         The sea for you is
murder "where the day drowns"
            "in whom the dead,
enwombed again cry out to us to return"
            For me it is
touching the source again,
          rubbing my body
against the seeds of beginning,
          core of renewal
     I must speak of fire as you do—for me,
breakdown of communication & the "secret joy" of
the others   "a defiance of authority . . . So be it."
     I beg to be taught
         & even by indirection
your shadow lengthening toward me,
          —of this, make it of *this*.

The Sea Inside

Those afternoons,
                the hot wind
                                & the striped
Mediterranean-colored curtains flapped & curvetted
in the doorway,   rearing
to let the air in, the lifted roar
of waves,
                their down-crashing,
                                turning
our bodies to each other, reaching
for what we blindly found   (to hold)
                                eyes closed,
every pore opened to know the other's
skin, nails, sweat, hair, saliva,
                        bodies
locked, twined, interlaced   to breathe
the sea inside us,
                the heaving,   the waywardness
out of the other's breath

Between Now and the Red Sea

The sea I swam in at Eilath
is a bivalve:
              there is a depth on it
facing two ways at
once.
       It is hollowed out by a
weight.
       The darkness of it is an
eloquence in a still partly
unknown language.
              It raises me up and
moves me
between now and the Red Sea, between
Israel and
Egypt.

White Snake

Give birth to yourself, he said,
                                    over
30 years ago
                And years later
there was that dream,   dream of
a white snake coiling & uncoiling
beside a rock.
                It is the snake of
                life, D. told me,
her eyes smiling: It is of life, not
death.   The snake shedding
his skin, is born
again & again & white is
the color of renewal.
                        Now (much later)
                        the hills dip roundly here.
They make enormous curves,
                                    heaving
softly,   swelling in heaviness
                                    & larger
than any human curves, male or
female
            (but a Hindu goddess
            might possess them)
Last night it was these mountains
that heaved,
                shining
under the moon,   in a light intensely
brilliant
            Today the hills dove
deeply,
            below the roots of trees,
            aiming at
those wedges between valleys.
                                All day the wind has battered
at the sun,
            light pressed
against the fog,
                grey swirling & covering
the blue.
            These ridges folded
on each other touch in
intensity. They bulk insistently:
                                speaking to the sky,

they raise their heads.
                        These weeks & months
the green will cover them
                        Before they shed that skin
the young deer, moving in a delicate dance-step
which lifts them off the ground
                                & the hawk,   calmly sailing
with no wing moving   & making
the air his own,   will hear a watery sound in
this dry country,
                    will see it all
beginning again.

A Tree Planted

They tore my clothes
                 & said to me:
Don't be afraid—
                & I thought: tear them
& I one of that long line of women
mourning their beloved
dead three thousand
years,
       she with her mouth gaping, eyelids
purple-black.
         Don't be afraid, the woman said,
It's your mother.
          And they chanted
in His praise, blessing
the Lord, ruler
of the universe,   who does
justice also,
         covering,
covering her with shovelfuls
of earth.
       A sunny,
cool day & a light wind
blowing in our faces,
             the bougainvillea
red & glowing,
         trees greening
as in early spring,
         the earth,
the freshly-dug earth covering
the stiff small body of her who had
said earlier:
         I want you
to go & rest.
         I want to
kiss you but perhaps we shouldn't—
with this illness.
         I want you to
go home safely,
         to go to
the country to rest.
           I love you (but this only
              on the telephone)
I want a tree planted,
         a tree with flowers

on it"
          & then "Cover
my feet, they're cold. And make it
dark:
          close all the doors & give me
my burial-shroud—"
                    Little lioness,
under the dark earth, heavy
on that small body,
                    white with
that fire,
          burning,
burning in her pride.

The Whiteness

Deep, deep under white now I longed to be
& in the earth digging deep, to come alive
again,
        to find
a beginning
            & the late snow came,
in April,
          covering
the city,
         blotting out whatever
came before: the madman
gesticulating even on Fifth Avenue,
then vanishing
           & the lost men
in doorways, curled like embryos,
defenseless,
           & the women hunched
over shopping bags all
night: a white
sheet covers them,   an air of innocence,
a pause
       in which there is time still
to get ready,   time lost that
can be made up,
           under this covering,
this whiteness